Dear Ruth,
I would be honored if the words in this book helped you in your fundraising. Keep up the great work.
Wayne 11-3-2014

Planned giving is the only way
people can support your
organization that brings them
tremendous satisfaction, yet has
no impact on their lifestyle, other
than to improve it.

Wayne Olson

Also by Wayne Olson

Think Like a Donor

BIG GIFTS
SMALL EFFORT

Unleash Planned Giving's power for board members, development officers and everyone who wants to raise enough money to change their nonprofit forever.

For Heather, Nathan, Mark and to the great donors who have allowed me to become part of their families.

About the Author

Wayne Olson is one of the fortunate few who gets to do what he loves for a career. With a passion for explaining complicated ideas as simple concepts, he has served nonprofits and their supporters for more than a decade and a half.

An attorney by training and a television news producer before that, Wayne has served the latter half of his career as a planned giving director, trainer, leader and speaker for various nationwide nonprofits and charities.

His specialty is donor relations and how both nonprofits and for-profit corporations can engage donors and constituents in better ways.

Having served as an independent consultant and trainer, Wayne is the Director of Planned Giving for the University of the South and has served in planned giving roles with the American Cancer Society and the University of Richmond. He has taught planned giving, donor relations and presentation skills at the University of Richmond's School of Continuing Studies.

He is widely published having written for Crescendo Interactive's GiftLegacy for more than a decade. In the for-profit world, Wayne headed the Institutional Services department of The Trust Company of Virginia where he managed gift annuity programs and endowment management for several regional and national organizations.

Nationally, Wayne speaks on the subject of donor relations and planned giving and has presented numerous times to the Association of Fundraising Professionals conferences, and to Crescendo Practical Planned Giving Conferences. He is a frequent contributor to *Planned Giving Today*. He has twice been interviewed in the *Chronicle of Philanthropy*.

Wayne is also the author of the book, *Think like a Donor*, now in its fourth printing.

Acknowledgment

No one enters college or law school with the thought of graduating as a planned giving officer; at least no one I have met. Planned giving is learned along the way.

I am grateful to have encountered many kind mentors who took time to teach me about planned giving and donor relations. My hope is this book helps others as so many helped me.

To Fred who gave me my first job, thank you for emphasizing the importance of listening to the customer and giving the customer, and now *donor*, the best. It was Fred's teaching and leadership at Busch Gardens that continues to inspire.

To Ed, whose friendship reveals the importance of perseverance and continual learning, thank you. You embody the spirit of "never give up, never stop learning."

To Rob, whose invaluable friendship spans decades, thank you. No one reaches out or listens better than you. Few people genuinely care enough to simply call and ask, "What's going on?" and mean it!

To Eileen, Jay, Dick, Doug, Charles, Ardis, Kristen, Johnny, Tom, Bob and all my current and former leaders: you have my gratitude for every career success that has come or is yet to arrive. I hope to honor your gifts with my own giving.

To the countless charities, organizations and foundations that invited me to speak, present and coach, you teach me more than you know. I am honored that you put your faith and trust in me.

And to Nancy and Katie, this book is a result of our teamwork. Thank you for your expertise, collaboration and vision.

Finally, to you the reader, and to those who have heard me speak or have read my work in other media, thank you. The words in this book are a result of your kind encouragement.

Table of Contents

Foreword

Wayne Olson is one of the most dynamic, imaginative, and effective professionals working in the field of philanthropy today. His specialty is planned giving, and he takes this subject, which, in some instances can cause the eyes to glaze over, and makes it come alive. Not only that, but he also is able to make the complicated simple and, what is more, both relevant and attainable. These are rare qualities in a field that sometimes seems to have more than its share of those who borrow your watch to tell you what time it is.

Step by step, clearly and compellingly, Wayne Olson penetrates what can seem, to the untutored, holy mysteries. He explains the many ways in which an organization can maximize its fundraising capability and, more important, enable a donor to do more that he or she had ever thought possible.

The pages that follow will encourage readers to "unleash the power of planned giving." Planned giving is, indeed, powerful, and in the capable narrative of Wayne Olson, its potential is fully realized. As competition for the philanthropic intensifies, those who take the time to learn from Wayne Olson will find themselves, and their organizations, possessing a great advantage. This book is most timely and most welcome.

John M. McCardell, Jr.
Vice-Chancellor, The University of the South
Sewanee, Tennessee
April 2, 2014

Introduction

Planned Giving

Many people have heard of the term but few understand its meaning. Planned Giving is a gift to a nonprofit organization that will occur in the future. Planned gifts are typically found in wills, trusts, gift annuities and life insurance. But they can be made in numerous other ways as well.

A supervisor once told me a planned gift is any gift that takes more than two minutes to accomplish. While not the most scientific of explanations, it works. Perhaps the most important thing about planned gifts is that they are often large and come from your most dedicated supporters. An organization that can create and sustain a good planned giving program is one that will thrive and excel for years to come.

You Can Do It

Depending on whom you ask, and what source you rely on, planned giving results in an average gift of $40,000. Some suggest the number is higher. While planned giving does not get as much attention as other forms of fundraising, it is the secret (or not-so-secret) source for life-sustaining funds for a nonprofit.

Certainly if you read the names on buildings at colleges and universities, or at the head of public broadcasting television programs, you will see that planned gifts make a difference; a big difference.

> *If your nonprofit is not actively encouraging planned gifts, you are missing the single biggest source of revenue you could possibly attain for your organization.*

Other than the large numbers of dollars that come from planned gifts, there is another important way they are different than all other forms of giving.

Planned Giving is a Promise

Planned giving is a promise a donor makes to give something (usually money) to a nonprofit at a time in the future. Yet it is equally, if not more so, a promise from the nonprofit to the donor that it will perform its mission with care and respect for the donation.

I begin this book with a promise *to you*.

You Can Do It

I want you to succeed at planned giving. I want you to see that with just a little effort, you can facilitate, help create and fulfill the completion of many planned gifts for your cause.

While this book should prove helpful for new planned giving officers, its primary purpose is to aid Development Directors, Major Gift Officers, board members, pastors, and anyone else who can and should benefit from the many opportunities that planned giving provides for nonprofits.

Big Gifts do Come from Just a Small Effort

This book is organized around the simple proposition that *you can do it*. I want to begin by letting you know and by reminding myself, that you do not need to be an expert in planned giving, taxation, or estate planning to effectively and abundantly bring planned gifts to your cause.

Effective planned giving involves only three steps:

> 1. Advocate for your cause (be mission minded).
> 2. Make it easy for people to give.
> 3. Respect and thank those who do.

While this book touches on all three parts of this formula, you will find the main emphasis is on number two. Expand your fundraising by accepting and seeking more gifts by going beyond the simple cash gift or fundraising event.

You don't Need to be an Expert

Incorporating planned giving into fundraising does not have to be difficult. When I hire planned giving staff, or train planned giving officers for other charities, I am on the lookout for sincerity, authenticity and dedication to the mission, not necessarily technical proficiency. You can teach planned giving. You cannot train sincerity.

Donors Give to Sincere People
They do not Give to Technical Specialists

Loyalty to mission and fidelity to the cause are the most important determiners of planned giving success. If you have those, you have everything. Without it, this book can't help you.

While knowledge is always good, you don't need to be an expert in planned giving other than in two areas: being a good listener and knowing how to use available resources to help donors, and who to call for help when you lack resources. It helps to also always be willing to learn more.

I am always amazed when I talk with charities around the country (even large ones, by the way) who tell me they do not have time for planned giving, or they need the money *now* and "can't afford" to wait.

The reality is income from planned gifts towers over all others. Results from a dedication to planned giving can start showing immediately. Moreover, numerous studies have demonstrated that when a person makes a planned gift to your organization, all other types of giving from that donor typically increase as well.

Planned Giving is the Single Best Way
to Raise a lot of Money for Your Non-Profit

Unfortunately there are many people who do not understand planned giving. Even more disturbing: they are eager to share what they "know," with you! My hope is to show how simple planned giving can be. I will demonstrate how you can raise a lot of money with planned giving, without having to put too much effort into it. Along the way, I hope to dispel some of the other myths and misconceptions about planned giving.

Practical, not Academic

My goal is to help you and your nonprofit raise more money through planned gifts. However, my goal is *not* to make you an expert on planned giving, or go into great, unnecessary depth on specific planned gift details. My sole purpose is to help you raise more money for your organization's mission because it deserves it and because your donors have told you so.

A few notes as we move forward.

Charity

I use the words "charity," and "nonprofit," interchangeably. When you read either of these words, I am referring to an organization that has received a letter from the IRS recognizing it as a "qualified" nonprofit organization under either §501(c)(3) or §170 of the Internal Revenue Code. By the way, the "§" in that sentence is shorthand for "section." You may see this from time to time. I did not know what it was until I saw it in law school. If you did not know what it was before, you will now when you see it.

A Disclaimer

When I speak on planned giving and fundraising I often hear that planned giving and fundraising intimidates many people, even those who have dealt with it for a career for years.

I also see too many charities struggling, spending one dollar to raise 99 cents. *Big Gifts Small Effort*'s goal is to introduce the topic to those who want to learn more about it. Success will be measured by board members, fundraisers and donors wanting to learn more about this subject and start raising more money for the charity. The plan is to demystify planned giving. There are more complex, more detailed treatises on planned giving and the author encourages you to read them. Learn from them. It is in that spirit that I must emphasize and remind the reader: don't do what you don't know.

Find experts, get to know them and engage them. As you do, you will increase your knowledge and your comfort level. You will find your thirst for knowledge about planned giving will be quickly quenched with more donations, deeper relationships and an overall improving health for your nonprofit.

A Word about Words

If I use terms that sound clinical or insensitive, it is in the interest of economy of print and use of your time. Rather than spend a paragraph getting around to a point, I prefer to get to the heart of the matter right away.

It should be fairly obvious that I cherish my relationships with donors, love their dedication and literally owe my livelihood to them. As long as we all understand the donor comes first, we can go forth and talk frankly about terms such as death, big gifts, and impact without spending inordinate amounts of time trying to disguise the reality of how things work.

Chapter 1   Planned Giving

The Freight Train of Charitable Giving

- Planned Giving and the Big Gifts
- It is Easier than You Might Think
  - Getting Started

Why Planned Giving?

When people ask me about planned giving, I explain it as the freight train of charitable giving. If you were expecting a full shipment of gold, and the volume of gold was measured by the vehicle that brings it, which vehicle would be the most exciting to you: a cab, truck, plane or train?

It could be delivered by cab. Cabs are great for going small distances in a hurry. There's always another cab around the corner and you might use one or two of them in a relatively short period of time.

However cabs are not good for hauling much. They solve short-term needs and get you (and the gold) from Point A to Point B as long as the points are not too far apart. They are also expensive. They can cost several dollars per mile, and they are often messy, smelly, and require extra effort to ensure the cab goes exactly where you want it to go. Cabs are the special events of fundraising.

How about by truck? Trucks carry more freight than a car or cab, and can navigate streets fairly easily. Yet, freight often comes damaged, and trucks can be fairly expensive to run and maintain. Most importantly, trucks can be victims of timing. Rush hour, weather, toll roads and congestion at the loading dock can all hamper gold shipped by truck.

Trucks are the annual fund of charitable giving. When an annual fund response rate of 2% is considered phenomenal, there is a lot of overhead necessary to deliver gifts by truck. A lot falls off along the way.

Jet planes are wonderful. They can carry even more freight than a truck. They look gorgeous and have a sex appeal like no other form of transportation. When a jet arrives with someone (or something) special everyone knows about it. It makes news. However, while jets could carry your gold shipment, there is only so much weight a jet can carry. Unexpected weather, a limited number of runways and other factors can delay arrivals for a long time. More importantly, jets are particularly dependent on the skill and competence of the pilot or gift officer. One slip and the plane goes down. That makes news, too. Jets are the major gifts of fundraising.

Planned gifts are freight trains. They have been around for a long time. They are not as nimble as cars or trucks, and they lack the streamlined good looks of jets. Yet they are dependable. And they haul freight, lots and lots of freight – reliably and on time. Surprises in the weather, personnel or seasonal variables rarely affect freight arriving by train. Trains also deliver large quantities of goods for pennies a mile, cheaper than all other forms of transportation. Freight trains get the job done. Why pin your big hopes on cars, trucks and planes, when your train could be just around the bend? Take the train.

All Aboard Planned Giving

Planned giving is the freight train because it is so easy for people to use it to move large gifts.

With planned giving you can use almost any asset you have. You can't use a diamond ring to pay for a ticket to a ball or gala, but you can leave it in your will to charity. Similarly, stocks, real estate, vehicles, vessels, artwork, and cash can be the subject of a planned gift. Best of all planned giving offers many options to the donor.

Real property, for example, could be transferred to one of several trusts that are designed to own real property. The donor receives benefits for a specified time, then the property, or a portion of it, can go to your cause. When you give someone options, they give more...because they can.

One of the joys of planned giving is the delight of opening new opportunities for the donor. It could be showing the donor a way of making a donation to charity and getting cash back. Perhaps it is the happy look on the donor's face when you tell the donor that the highly appreciated stock which had been a tax burden can be a blessing when used to fund a gift.

Undoubtedly though, the most rewarding aspect of planned giving is that anyone of any means can make a meaningful gift. Whether by will, trust or gift annuity, planned giving opens doors for donors that most donors never knew existed.

Planned Giving's Value

Planned giving is the best measure of an organization's fiscal well-being. A good planned giving program is a sign of a healthy nonprofit. A poor or nonexistent planned giving program is a reliable indicator that the nonprofit is struggling with money and may not be around long.

When donors choose to make a planned gift to your organization they have said they value your cause as much as they do their family or closest friends. Planned giving donors are telling you they trust you to spend their money just as they would spend it, even though they know they will never be able to watch you do so. That says a lot.

And just like family, when we surround ourselves with people who care that deeply in us and invest emotionally in us; we endure. You cannot fail when people identify with you and would do anything in partnership with you. Planned giving also provides your nonprofit with the sustaining funds it needs to keep it going for a long time.

How Simple can Planned Gifts be?

A planned giving program does not have to be complicated to be effective. You can achieve remarkable results by adding words such as the following to the footer of your stationary or in a small ad in your newsletter: "Please remember to include [our organization, tax ID Number XX-XXXXX] in your will, trust, or estate plan."

With the average planned giving bequest in the tens of thousands of dollars, if only one person reads your ad and follows it, you have increased your bottom line significantly. If two follow it or three.... you have successfully changed the long-term health of your organization.

Planned Gifts Take Many Forms

A good planned giving program includes any type of giving to a nonprofit other than cash. Think of these as tools to work with your donors and advisors to build the gift that works best for them and your nonprofit.

In the following pages, the gift vehicles are listed first, and then each will be examined in detail:

- Wills

- Trusts

- Charitable Gift Annuities

- Life Insurance

- IRAs (and other retirement plans)

All of these planned gifts can be funded with cash, check, or other assets such as:

- Stock (both publicly traded and closely-held)

- Real property (homes, farms and forests)

- Art, jewelry, vehicles, vessels and other personal property

With a few variations any type of planned gift can be funded with just about any type of asset.

This reason alone gives you, the nonprofit fundraiser, the ability to do so much more than simply ask for another $20 check for the latest sale, rally or run. Planned giving gives donors options. These options help donors give more because they now have a variety of ways to give.

Planned Giving is about Unlimited Opportunities

Planned giving opens an enormous world of opportunity, not just for the nonprofit, but also for the donor. The charity benefits from sizeable and more frequent gifts than it would otherwise not receive, and the donor converts what might be a burdensome asset into a generous gift. The donor receives a significant tax benefit, and when done properly, *even cash back*. You cannot beat planned giving for its pure efficiency and abundance of value to donors and nonprofits.

Just by embracing planned giving, your nonprofit will benefit immediately. Donors will see your commitment to them extends beyond the next event, beyond the next budget cycle. Their gift has a lasting, important philanthropic effect on a cause meaningful to them. You will see gifts emerge you might never have expected.

As you read on, ideas should jump off the page that inspire you to call one of your donors with a recommendation that helps him or her right away. If you are a board member or donor yourself, perhaps you will call your gift officer with some ideas of your own.

As you venture forward into the world of planned giving, seek opportunities. Explore options. Search for ways to **serve** donors with creative ideas and inventive techniques. Importantly, as you learn about different ways of making planned gifts work, take a lesson from your donors: let your heart lead the way and allow your instincts to guide you. While the technical aspects are important and the skills will take you far, it is how you use them and where you take them that matters.

Those Who Avoid Planned Giving Don't Know Planned Giving

An unfortunate misconception about planned giving is that it is about death and dying. Perhaps it is this association of planned giving that intimidates most charities. Who wants to talk about dying? The answer is: no one. But the reality is planned giving is not about a death. It is about a life.

A planned gift conveys this message: *I want to live every day knowing I am going to do something good for you, or with you.* It is not about dying, although we all die. It is not depressing, although you can make it that way.

"And how we deal with death is at least as important as how we deal with life, wouldn't you say?" – Captain James T. Kirk

Planned giving is not about the event of death; it is about the meaning of life. Planned gifts are often huge. The emotion we invest in our donors is reflected in the dollars they invest in us.

The good news for you is that there are probably plenty of people already in love with your mission and already wanting to make a planned gift to you; they just need you to open the door for them and invite them to step in.

Think of the many possibilities for a donor when you can use all kinds of assets the donor has in various combinations to do good for the donor and for the nonprofit.

You don't have to be a planned giving expert to be an expert fundraiser who happens to use planned giving effectively and powerfully to raise more money, much more money for your nonprofit.

To recap:

- Planned Giving Brings in Major Money

- Planned Giving Gives Donors Options

- It is Easy to Get Started

Chapter 2   Taxes

Incredible Benefits of Tax-Wise Giving

- Why Taxes Matter
- Some Tax Basics
- Types of Taxes

Some Tax Basics, Really Basic!

Any discussion of planned giving would be incomplete without at least a cursory look at taxes. They are an important part of planned giving.

Tax savings are the result of almost all planned giving strategies. While it is crucial to understand how taxes figure into planned giving, it is no less important to grasp the concept that no one ever makes a planned gift solely for tax reasons.

The United States did not have an income tax (as we know it today) until 1913. Yet, Americans were charitable before then and have been charitable since. While tax savings are an important aspect of nonprofit work, they are not the main reason why people give.

People make charitable gifts because they want to support a nonprofit organization. They want to make a difference in the world around them, and they believe your organization presents the best opportunity to make that difference for them.

Tax savings or tax benefits are a worthy byproduct or a secondary reason for giving. While taxes are not the primary reason for giving, they are a reason. To raise money through planned gifts, you should have a basic understanding of taxes. They need not be mastered.

Our role is never to provide tax advice. Rather, our role is to look out for donors so we can point to ways of giving more strategically. We are expected to be *mission experts*, not *tax experts*.

Gain a basic understanding of taxes and a thorough appreciation for the concept that, "The things we don't know that we don't know can be dangerous." No matter how much we learn about taxes we will never know as much as those who work with taxes all day, every day.

I heard a planned giving expert once say the day a wealthy person looks to the zoo for tax advice is the same day the zoo looks for an accountant to feed the animals. The point is we should learn about taxes so we know smart questions to give donors to ask their tax advisors.

Quid Quo Pro - the Only Latin You Need to Know

When you give a gift to charity your gift should be your gift and your deduction should be your deduction and your deduction should be equal to your gift. It's a long sentence, that if reduced to a math equation would look something like this:

$$Deduction = Gift.$$

Historically, while that was pretty much the case pretty much all the time, it wasn't always and isn't always today.

There was a time when you could give $50 for a gala and take a $50 income tax deduction even though you enjoyed a lobster dinner at the gala worth $40. The IRS caught on (author's note: rightfully so) and those days are long gone.

Today when a donor receives something of value or even the right to receive something of value from a donation, then the gift value of the contribution is reduced by that amount.

This is most commonly related to items such as event tickets, meals, football games, and similar outings. While they typically don't apply to the planned giving realm, it is helpful to know about this rule and remember that donors should never receive anything of value in return for a donation. When the donor does, the donor should be made aware of what that value is and the nonprofit should appropriately document the receipt. Items of minimal value such as key chains and t-shirts are okay to distribute freely.

When is the Gift Made?

No Matter how large a gift is, it is important to be accurate when recording when the gift is made. Below is a chart to help you record gift dates properly.

Method of Gift	Date of Gift
Hand Delivery (in person):	Date charity takes possession
U.S. Mail:	Postmark on envelope*
UPS and Federal Express:	Date charity takes delivery
Credit Card:	Date donor authorizes payment
Electronic Transfer:	Date completed by bank
Stock (paper certificates):	Date charity takes possession of endorsed certificates
Stock (brokerage account):	Date charity receives transfer of shares in its account

*Note that it is the postmark on the envelope and not the date the charity receives it. The donor can mail the check on December 31 and the charity receive it January 3 and the gift counts as December 31 as long as the postmark is December 31.

How Much is that Stock Worth?

When a donor gifts shares of stock, how much are they worth? Stock prices change moment by moment. Is it the value when the donor ordered the broker to sell it? Is it the value when it appeared in your organization's account? The answer is: neither.

When a donor makes a stock gift for any reason (whether an outright gift or for a gift annuity or other planned gift) the value of the stock is the average of the high and low selling price on the day the stock enters the charity's brokerage account.

Your broker will let you know the stock has arrived. Ask what the high and low for the stock was that day, calculate the average, and then multiple by the number of donated shares to determine the gift value.

Let the donor know ahead of time that this is how the donation will be valued, especially if the donor is thinking about "timing" the donation. It simply cannot be done; at least not within less than a couple days of certainty. Sometimes this works in the donor's favor, sometimes in the charity's favor. This occurs especially when funding charitable gift annuities. Keep everyone informed every step of the way and make sure your illustrations and contracts are up to date and accurate. Remember, too, the donor will have to supply you with the cost basis for this stock donation (more about that later).

There are Limits to Everything

The IRS does not want the party to go on forever, so it puts a limit on how much individual taxpayers can give to charity in a given year.

While each deduction may be totally deductible, the most a donor can deduct in a given year is 50% of the donor's Adjusted

Gross Income. If a donor's Adjusted Gross Income is $100,000, then the most the donor can deduct is $50,000 even if the donor gave everything away to charity. The good news is the donor can "carry over" any unused charitable deduction for up to five additional years.

The most a donor can deduct for gifts of appreciated property is 30% of Adjusted Gross Income. When the donor gives both cash and long-term appreciated property, the cash is counted first, followed by the appreciated property.

Any giving that exceeds 50% of Adjusted Gross Income or any Appreciated Assets that exceed 30% of Adjusted Gross Income may be carried over for up to five years.

Keep it Real, Know Your Limits

Don't feel fooled or feel pressure to be an expert on taxes. Yes, it helps to know the Federal Tax Code, and yes, you will inevitably learn about taxes as you progress with planned gifts, but think about this: donors do *not* expect you to be an expert on taxes. They expect people their accountants to be the experts. You can only offer guidance and provide questions for the donor to take to experts.

If you feel intimidated, remember this: if you provide legal or tax advice to a donor, you are practicing law without a license. With increasing knowledge and experience you can point out areas for the donor to ask questions to the professionals. You do not have to be an expert on anything other than your mission!

Even if you are an accountant or attorney, you cannot advise the donor and the charity; that is a conflict of interest if you work for a charity or represent it as a volunteer.

Public Charities

This book is designed to cover situations most of us will encounter, specifically situations involving public charities. Public charities are those the IRS recognizes under §501(c)(3) or §170. There are other organizations such as private foundations with slightly different rules, which, while very similar, are not the same.

If your family has established a foundation, or you work for a private foundation, ask your counsel for specific differences between planned giving for public and private charities. The main way these differences show up is in the limits it places on the deductions available to donors.

Let's talk about taxes and what you need to know, and what you don't need to know.

The United States
Taxes Income, not Wealth

First, let's dispel a common misunderstanding about taxes. In the United States, *we do not tax wealth*. We tax *income*. We tax the movement of money, not the holding of it.

> *Whether your net worth is $5, $500,000, or*
> *$5 million, but you earn no money this year,*
> *you owe no income taxes.*

Even experienced gift officers, when soliciting gifts and pointing out the tax savings, often forget that some of our wealthiest citizens pay little income taxes each year, because they made little income. As we explore taxes together and as you talk about them with donors, remember that "wealth" does not always translate into the need for tax relief. Income does.

The Truth about Tax Brackets

Have you ever heard people say they would not want a pay raise because it would "put them in a higher tax bracket?" While it's true they might be in a higher tax bracket, that is not a good reason to turn down the raise.

Let's say the tax rates look like this:

$10,000+   = 20% rate
$20,000+   = 30% rate
$30,000+   = 40% rate

If you make, for example, $20,000 a year, you pay 20% on your first $10,000 of salary and 30% on the second $10,000, or a total of $5,000 in taxes. You would not pay 30% on all of your salary!

If you are making $29,999 and get a $5,000 raise, the higher tax bracket of 40% applies only to the salary you receive over $30,000. Your salary goes up by $5,000, and your taxes increase by $2,000. That's a lot of taxes, but not as much as if you paid 40% on your total salary.

Our system is set up on a *graduated scheme*. Everyone pays the same tax on the same amount of money. If the tax rate for $0-$30,000 is 10%, then everyone in the country pays 10% on the first $30,000 of income. If the next bracket has a rate of 15%, then everyone pays 15% on money earned over $30,000. You only pay the higher rate when you cross an earnings threshold (or bracket) and even then only pay the higher amount on that part of your income above the bracket threshold.

Active and Passive Taxation

Income taxes take two forms. Each is taxed differently. There is active income and there is passive income.

Active Income

Active income is the money you earn when you go out and work for it; when you do something yourself. Active income is what most people typically think of when it is time to pay taxes. This income also includes interest you earn on savings, and income from rents or royalties.

Passive Income

Passive income is, in its most basic form, when your money makes money for you. It usually occurs when you sell something for more than you paid for it. For example, that stock your grandfather bought for $10 is now worth $100. When he goes to sell it, he will pay capital gains tax on the $90 gain.

Note that he is paying tax on the gain, and not the total value of the stock. This is a common oversight when discussing taxes. Capital gains tax is exactly what it says it is. It is the tax you pay *on the gain* your capital (cash) has made since you invested it, which is almost always different than the sale price.

When Passive is Active

If you own something less than a year and sell it, it is not taxed as a capital gain, it is taxed at your income tax rate which is often much higher. Any asset held less than a year before it is sold, is considered a short-term capital gain, and is taxed as ordinary income.

How Charitable Giving Affects Taxes

When a donor does take advantage of a charitable income tax deduction, it means the donor can reduce income by the amount contributed to charity. If the donor reports $100,000 in income and has income tax deductions totaling $30,000, the donor will pay income tax as if he or she earned only $70,000 and not $100,000. Said another way, the donor will pay as a donor would in the $70,000 tax bracket.

The Standard Deduction

Congress allows a standard deduction. The standard deduction varies with inflation and with congressional action, but is essentially an automatic tax deduction. Without ever giving a nickel to charity (or paying interest on your mortgage – which is another popular tax deduction), you can opt to take the standard deduction and get a deduction anyway.

Unless a person is really charitable and gives above and beyond what the standard deduction offers automatically, even the income tax deductions associated with charitable giving do not help the donor. Donors who give beyond the allowed standard deduction itemize their deductions because they choose to list their donations item-by-item, rather than taking the standard deduction.

Taxes on the Movement of Wealth

There are other types of federal taxes that are far less common because they apply to fewer of us. Those types of taxes are on transfers of wealth. These most commonly take the form of gift, estate, and generation skipping taxes. Even though in most cases, income taxes have already been paid on all funds subject to these taxes, the government will tax your ability to move your money to someone else by taxing transfers between people.

Whether wealth is distributed a little at a time or a bunch of it upon death, the government can take a share of it with these three forms of taxes. Gifts you make to other people during life are subject to the gift tax. If your estate is big enough, you'll pay estate taxes. If you transfer assets to your grandchildren, generation skipping taxes are paid.

Estate Tax

The estate tax, also known as the death tax, applies only to a minimal number of taxpayers as the law stands today. When it does apply to an estate, it can take a huge bite out of that estate. However, the reality is less than one percent of Americans are subject to the estate tax. As of this writing any estate over $5.34 million is subject to estate taxes and can be taxed at rates up to 40%.

However, this tax and its rates have been changing in recent years and is subject to debate this year and for the foreseeable future. Check with your counsel or planned giving software provider to learn what the current rates are. You don't need to know this for any reason other than to learn the motivations your donor might have in giving to your nonprofit in a tax-wise way.

Gift Tax

The Gift Tax works closely with the Estate Tax and together the two regulate transfers of wealth between individuals. The basic idea is that one taxes transfers during life, while the other taxes transfers after death. Together, they make sure individuals cannot give money to others without passing through an IRS filter. It is because of these two taxes that planned giving becomes more attractive.

The estate and gift tax work together so that, for example, when someone realizes death is approaching they cannot give everything away while still alive to beat the death tax.

The Gift Tax applies to all transfers of money. The IRS says the general rule is that any gift is a taxable gift. However, the IRS also points out exceptions:

- Gifts that are no more than the *annual exclusion* for the calendar year.

- Tuition or medical expenses you pay on behalf of someone else.

- Gifts to your spouse.

- Gifts to a political organization for its use.

Gift Tax Exclusions

Notice the first bullet point above? Annual exclusion? Each year the government determines a sum of money you can give away to an individual without paying the gift tax. The annual exclusion is (at this moment) $14,000 but is likely to change. As a practical matter, you can give $14,000 this year to each child and not pay gift taxes on the gifts.

You could give this amount to strangers too. The basic idea is the government limits individuals to a certain amount of giving to other individuals to $14,000 each year. There is no limit on how many people you can give money. Should you wish to experience the joy of giving money to someone other than a child and not pay gift tax, you can send me $14,000 in care of my publisher. I promise to write you a very nice thank you note.

Some Thoughts on Gift Taxes

Whenever a donor talks about including someone other than himself or herself as a beneficiary of a planned gift, bells and whistles should go off in your mind to be extra careful. Fortunately, your planned giving software should catch this for you, if you complete the donor and beneficiary sections of the program properly.

Donors may have tough tax burdens with estate and gift taxes that prevent them from freely giving money to family and friends. This is true whether they try to give away money during life or at death. And donors are obligated to keep track of all money they give away, and if not subject to one of the exceptions or exclusions, they must pay gift or estate tax on those transfers.

The gift tax also comes into play with charitable giving. When we establish a gift annuity for a donor who designates someone other than the spouse as the beneficiary, there is a chance the gift forming the annuity is subject to gift tax.

Generation Skipping Tax

Related to the Gift and Estate tax is yet another tax, the Generation Skipping Tax. The Generation Skipping Tax only applies to very large estates. Its purpose is to prevent the very wealthy from avoiding other taxes by leaving large amounts to grandchildren.

In theory, if the money is left to the immediate next generation, the children, there would be another level of taxes payable before the children passed the money on to grandchildren.

By "skipping" a generation, taxpayers might be able to also skip that level of taxation. Again, the tax applies only to the wealthiest among us. Some planned giving vehicles (the Charitable Lead Trust, in particular) are available to help lessen the blow of this tax.

Taxes and Giving

"The tax code is now nine times longer than
the Bible, and not nearly as interesting." –
Rob Portman

Depending on the size of the paper on which it is printed, the U.S. Tax Code is about 75,000 pages long.

Even tax code *reform* results in more complexity. You should know this because as a gift officer you might never know or appreciate the subtleties as much as someone who practices the Tax Code every day. Even then, ask ten tax attorneys a question about anything other than the simplest question and you are likely to get ten different answers.

Planned gifts affect taxes in two ways. They can reduce the annual income and capital gains taxes a donor pays. They can reduce the gift, estate, or generation-skipping taxes the donor, or the donor's heirs, will pay. Often, a planned gift can eliminate or reduce both income and estate taxes.

While taxes are never the primary reason for a donor to give to your organization, they are a reason, and it is worth knowing the basics of each type. Income taxes, capital gains taxes, gift taxes, estate taxes, and generation skipping taxes are real taxes with real bite.

While all but income taxes and capital gains taxes apply only to the very wealthy, they do apply. And since the premise of this book is to help you bring in big gifts, take the time to move beyond the basics. As we talk about different assets available for planned gifts, and different ways of making a planned gift, we'll examine how each one can impact each of these taxes.

To Recap:

- Planned gifts reduce income taxes, death taxes and almost every other type of tax.

- While the estate and gift taxes are formidable, they only affect a small percentage of Americans.

- Most Americans take the Standard Deduction, meaning a charitable tax deduction is of no use for them, tax-wise.

- The sale of an asset held less than one year is subject to ordinary income tax rates, not capital gains rates.

- Any gift to charity reduces the donor's estate by some if not all of the amount of the donation. And if the estate is reduced, that means less of the estate would be subject to estate tax, if it were subject to the tax at all.

Chapter 3   Wills

Where Big Gifts Live

- Boring or Exciting – It's How You Look at It
  - How Wills Work, and Don't Work
    - To Know Wills is to Love Wills

Boring or Exciting – it's how You Look at it

Let's start our discussion about wills with some important points. Wills are not sexy. They are not really exciting. They don't happen quickly, and even once they are written, testators (persons executing the wills) can change them.

> "One of the deep secrets of life is
> that all that is really worth doing is
> what we do for others." – Lewis Carol

So why bother to talk about them? Only one reason: there is no better way to raise large sums of money for your cause or organization than through wills. While other types of giving are more exciting and get more attention, wills get the job done. It is *always true* that a donor can afford to give more to you through a will than with any other type of giving.

> *The donor can give much more to your*
> *organization by will because it has zero*
> *impact on the donor's lifestyle!*

With all cash gifts and almost all other types of gifts, the donor has to choose between keeping the money, using it as the donor wants to use it, or giving it up. By giving $100 to your cause, the donor can no longer spend that money on dinner, gas, movies or books. It is gone.

However, when the donor has the option of giving money by will, it is a much easier decision. It is no longer a choice between the donor going out to eat or to the movie. It is a choice between leaving the money to family or friends, or as might be the case, choosing between giving the money to the government through taxes or to your cause.

Wills are about Legacies and Leaving a Mark on Life

During this discussion of wills and all planned gifts, the text will be matter-of-fact. It might come across as being cold about the subject. It is not. Rather than try to dance around the facts and issues, I would rather get to the point about what you need to know. Accordingly, this and all chapters will be practical. Your time is important. I honor that.

It is a terrible disservice, however, to talk about wills (and trusts) in purely economic terms. Wills are about legacy, making a difference, and creating a bond between charity and donor that goes beyond a simple financial transaction. In this chapter, we'll discuss the thinking of donors and why wills are such an attractive way to give. We'll also look at ways of making gifts by will more appealing for your donors and would-be donors.

First, we'll look at wills from a nonprofit's point of view – and why they should be a big part of your program. For all the major nonprofit organizations in this country, planned giving forms the bulk of their funding. Of all planned gifts, bequests bring in the most money.

What Exactly is a Will?

Remember, your job is not to write the donor's estate plan. Your job is to help the donor fulfill the donor's philanthropic goals in collaboration with and as a part of your organization's mission. I will give you insights and ideas that some of the most seasoned professionals lack. You can learn a lot about wills in a short time, and more than enough to be an effective planned giving fundraiser.

Let's start with some basic concepts and terminology about wills.

- A will is a document that lists the donor's wishes for the things the donor owns after the donor dies. This is one area where the word means what it says. It's all about the donor's "will" for the donor's possessions or assets. Almost all states require the will to be typewritten or printed. In those states, oral or handwritten wills are not valid.

- A bequest is a way of identifying a paragraph in the donor's will. For example, in a particular paragraph, sentence or clause in the will, the testator has a bequest for $10,000 to the ABC Organization (or to his daughter, Sally). That's a bequest. If a will was an essay, a bequest would be a key paragraph or sentence.

- A codicil is a revision to a will. A codicil can make a minor change to a will or make wholesale revisions. A charity can have a bequest in a codicil that is as valid as if it was in the existing will. While a new will replaces the old will in its entirety, a codicil only replaces or updates or adds to an existing will.

- An *estate plan* is the whole package. An estate plan could be a one page will, or it could involve trusts, gift annuities and could include a thirty-page will. The estate plan is not so much a written document as it is the donor/testator's overall plan for how to deal with every aspect of final wishes and disposition of assets. The best estate plans often include a will that's only one or two pages, because all assets have been transferred into trusts, life insurance, or other means.

- Beware of fundraisers who claim to want "irrevocable bequests." There is no such thing. During lifetime, a person can always change his or her mind. *Always.* Market conditions can double or eliminate wealth overnight. Treat all bequests as if they can change, because they can.

Your goal is for your nonprofit to be the recipient of a gift mentioned in a bequest in a will, or part of a trust, life insurance or some other way conveyed as part of a well thought-out estate plan.

How Wills Work

How does a will give something to charity? There are many ways, but they usually take one of the following forms. You will quickly become familiar with the following terms as you increase your knowledge about planned giving and wills.

- Specific bequest– A specific bequest is a gift in a will of a particular thing or asset. As with the word "will," this means exactly what it says. A donor devises (a fancy verb meaning "to give by will") something specific in a bequest. A specific devise could be a sum of money, such as "I give to ABC charity $10,000." A specific devise could be an object: "I give my 1953 Chevrolet Corvette, vehicle identification number 1234, to ABC Charity." A specific devise is any identifiable thing the donor owns and wants to give to you or anyone through a provision in a will. The problem with specific bequests is that the specific thing may no longer exist when the donor dies. If the donor sells the Corvette after making the will, there is no Corvette left to give you. States differ on the treatment of specific devises that are frustrated (another common word with a legal twist). Frustration means something that was intended, but is no longer possible. It is often heard as "frustration of purpose." A remedy might be to replace the item with cash, but only if available in the estate and if state law allows.

- Percentage bequest– This type of language devises a certain percentage to your charity. A donor could leave 1 percent, 2 percent or 99.5 percent to charity. It can be any percentage as long as it is practicable. One cannot leave, for example, one car to two people, especially when they live 500 miles apart. No one can drive half a car. Percentage bequests can be deceptive. They sound small, but a gift of "10 percent of my estate" to a nonprofit can equal a very nice gift.

- Contingent bequest– The donor has decided to give something to you only if other things happen first. A donor might state, "If my wife dies before me, and my children all die before me and all my grandchildren die before me, then I give 10 percent to ABC Charity." I threw in a percentage just to show how many variations there can be. It can be much more varied than this! Remember that a contingent bequest is real and it counts. Some strange contingencies have happened. The contingency usually is some assurance the family is taken care of and only then does money go to a secondary choice (often, but not always a charity). It could also be something as benign as, "I order my stock in XYZ Corporation be sold and the first $100,000 in proceeds be given to my son; any proceeds above $100,000 I give to ABC Charity."

- Remainder bequest– This is also known as a basket clause, or a residuary clause. The idea is to "catch" anything at the end or bottom of the will not already distributed. Wills usually begin with specific bequests and work down through contingent bequests, if any, and finally end with a remainder clause. Don't think of a remainder clause as meaning "leftovers." Technically, yes, a remainder bequest is the doggy bag of charitable giving. It is what's left. But a skilled attorney can be effective using a remainder clause to leave a great many assets to be disposed of by this clause, especially when the remainder beneficiary is a charity.

A Final Word about Words

With a little imagination, wills can be used to handle almost any donor need or concern. If a donor tells you he cannot give because he must care for his wife, you can respond with, "Have you ever thought about naming us as contingent beneficiary?" That's part of the beauty of planned giving: even those who think they can't give can find ways to give if they are open to the idea and that idea is properly introduced.

Sample Will Language

To receive a planned gift by will (or by trust), show the donor the way. You should work with your own board and counsel to develop sample will language to provide to your donors. Offer it when they call and ask for it. Use it in ads. Load it on your website. Make sure anyone can easily access it.

My only caution is to add a clear provision anywhere you give your language to the effect that "this language is provided to you so that with the help of your attorney you can provide for your gift to ABC Charity in your overall estate planning."

Feel free to change this wording (working with your attorney), but the goal is to remind your donor that these words alone are not enough. Only a qualified attorney can draft a will properly, especially when it includes a gift to charity.

Challenge your board members to include your organization in their wills for at least 2% of their estates. No child or family member will ever miss 2%, and if a board member is not willing to give 2%, maybe he or she should not be on the board.

So how about a starting point? Take the language below to your board and counsel and adopt it for your own organization's use. Just as I would tell a donor, *while this is good general language, you need to adopt it for your needs and your situation – and only a qualified attorney can help you do that.* With the understanding that this is only offered as a starting point for a discussion with your attorney; below is suggested language I have offered donors:

(Your Logo Here)

Below is suggested language; however, we encourage your attorney to amend it to suit your particular situation.

I give, devise and bequeath to ABC Charity, Inc., Tax Identification Number XX-XXXXXXX, the sum of $_____ (or state fraction or percentage of the estate) to be used for its general purposes. ABC Charity can be contacted in care of ABC Charity, Inc.'s office of Planned Giving, 1234 Main Street, City, State, ZIP code, Phone Number and www.abccharity.org.

There are key items I include in will language that I encourage you to also offer. The charity's Tax ID number is included because attorneys appreciate precision and it leaves no ambiguity. Include websites, email addresses and any contact information that helps the attorney probating the estate to find the charity and bring the gift to your organization.

There's another document you should have in your portfolio. It goes by various names, but I call it a Bequest Intention Form. This is simply a declaration from the donor to your organization, to formalize the idea that the donor has included your organization in the donor's will. Here's a sample for you to consider and redesign for your own purposes:

(Your logo)
ABC Charity
1234 Main Street
City, State ZIP Code
(XXX) XXX-XXXX (phone)
www.abccharity.org

Statement of Bequest Intention

I have provided a gift for ABC Charity as set forth in my will, trust, retirement plan or other estate plan.

The current estimated value of the gift is $_____. (Leave this blank for the donor to complete)

I understand this statement does not constitute a legally binding agreement.

My gift is unrestricted and to be used at the discretion of ABC Charity and its board of directors (yes) or (no) (circle one).

If "no," my gift is designated for the following uses (if more than one designation, please specify percentages or amounts to each):

_____

To ensure that my wishes are followed, I attach a relevant portion of my will or estate plan for ABC Charity's records and permanent file (optional).

Signed:

_____   _____
Donor   Date

_____
Donor's name printed

(Add another set of lines if more than one donor)

[If your organization has an honorary planned giving recognition society, offer the donor the opportunity to join it here]

ABC Charity [Honorary Planned Giving Society Name]

Please choose one:

____ Yes, please include me/us as member(s) of the ABC Charity Planned Giving Society; ABC Charity has my/our permission to publicly recognize my/our gift.

____ Yes, please include me/us as member(s) of the ABC Charity Planned Giving Society; but ABC Charity does not have my/our permission to publicly recognize my/our gift.

____ No, please do not include me/us as member(s) of the ABC Charity Planned Giving Society.

____ I wish to remain anonymous with this gift.

Please return to:

Planned Giving Officer
ABC Charity
1234 Main Street
City, State ZIP Code
(XXX) XXX-XXXX
www.abccharity.org
yourname@abccharity.org

Remembering that most planned giving donors are older, choose a font and font size that is easy for them to read and take to their attorney. I suggest sample will language (and all communications to donors) in at least 14 points! (The text in this paragraph is printed in 14 points)

- The suggested will language helps you and the donor shepherd the gift into formality. The will language is the key to help the donor's attorney draft the will (or other instrument) to properly include your organization.

- The Bequest Intention Form is useful for memorializing the gift and also in creating an official record for the files of your organization. Your board, if not your senior officers, will want proof the planned giving tree is going to produce fruit.

While this form never guaranties a gift will come in, it does help give at least some written evidence that it's a good possibility. Also, years from now, when the gift arrives, or should arrive, it helps to have something to match with the incoming gift.

Remember with planned giving, the donor is always in control. Whether the donor completes every form you provide or none of them, there is only one form that counts— the donor's will. It is our job to make that is as easy as possible for the donor to do; whether or not our tracking forms are completed.

Please know that many planned gifts arrive unexpectedly, emphasizing the importance of getting the word out. People can and will choose to include your organization in their plans without calling you. And many times people will sign bequest intention forms, but their plans or circumstances change.

Knowing this, it is good practice to maintain solid will language and offer it freely to donors to take to attorneys. Keep, update and use good bequest intention forms, so donors know you take their intentions seriously and will honor them when the time comes.

Why Things Go Wrongly

Unfortunately, I have seen attorneys draft wills that include gifts to "the animal shelter," or "my church." Twenty years after the will is written, how does the probating attorney (the one following the will) figure out which animal shelter it is? Which church? Was it the church the donor attended as a little girl and the next sixty years of her life, or the one she had been active in within her retirement home for the last seven years of her life?

Help the attorney leave no ambiguity. Make sure even the least experienced probating attorney can make no mistake in finding your organization to make sure the gift makes it to the right place—just as the donor intended.

Where there is a Will...

Wills are the powerhouses of charitable giving. Unfortunately, they do not receive nearly the recognition they deserve. It's hard to publicly recognize a donor for a promise to give, and when the gift is received the donor is the one person you cannot invite to the party! However, wills provide an opportunity for everyone of every means to give freely to your organization.

As fundraisers, it is our duty to get information to donors and to their counsels so they can make the gift properly. With experience, we can learn to listen for situations where a gift by will might be particularly attractive to a donor.

Using the will, and its variations, we can work with donors to create a perfect recipe for giving in a way that helps them achieve their goals, minimize taxes, and give in a way that does not affect their lifestyles. There is no other method of giving that offers so many opportunities and possibilities – and yet is so relatively simple.

To Recap:

- Wills are the most significant planned gift for dollars raised.

- A donor can make a large gift by will that the donor was never able to make during life.

- A donor or circumstances can always change a gift to be made by will.

- Make it easy for donors to include your organization in their wills by offering bequest language and honor that intention with bequest declaration forms you ask the donor to complete.

- Make sure donors give attorneys enough information about your organization so that many years from now the bequest is easy to understand and follow.

Chapter 4   Charitable Gift Annuities

The Gift that Keeps on Giving

- The Gift that Pays Donors Back
- What is a Charitable Gift Annuity?
- How to Inspire Donors to Complete Them

Gift Annuities Pay Money to Donors

Charitable gift annuities are one of the best tools a planned giving officer or any charity can have. Donors love them for the relatively high payment rates as well as the tax benefits. For charities, they are one of the few irrevocable planned gifts. Once funded, they cannot be amended or changed. This is unlike revocable gifts such as wills, which can always be changed by the donor. The ongoing nature of gift annuities also gives ample opportunities for donors to bond with charities. They create and sustain a powerful relationship between donor, gift officer and nonprofit.

A Simple Agreement between Charity and Donor

A gift annuity is a *contract* between a nonprofit and a donor where the nonprofit agrees to pay the donor a fixed payment every year for as long as the donor lives. The payment rate never changes once funded; no matter what the economy does.

A Brief History

Charitable gift annuities have been around a long time. Some say they started with colleges in New England. Others say the first gift annuity was with the American Bible Society in New York. No matter where they started, thousands of organizations offer them today.

Let's look at the example of the American Bible Society. It shows not only how long charitable gift annuities have been available, but also beautifully illustrates the concept. In 1831, The American Bible Society approached a donor, John Frey, of Palatine, New York.

Frey wanted to give the Society money for its mission, but he couldn't give as much as he would like to have given because he was also responsible for his sister's care. He agreed to give the Society $1,000 if it would pay his sister $70 each year for the rest of her life, no matter how long she lived. They agreed. They did, and have been issuing gift annuities since.

The Technical Side

Because of the nature of gift annuities, any discussion must entail some technicalities, but just a few. We'll take an overview of gift annuities that is just technical enough to prepare you to ask the right questions. We'll supply a few answers, but consider this a starting point only to launch you in the right direction.

Gift Annuities are a Split-Interest Gift

Gift annuities belong to a special type of transaction called a split-interest gift. A split-interest gift is exactly what it sounds like. There are two interests resulting from this gift: the charity's and the donor's. That's the split. The charity derives a benefit from this gift, and so too, does the donor.

When a gift annuity is funded, the donor gives the charity a sum of money. Unlike a cash gift where the charity can use the money as it wants, the incoming cash (or other asset) for a gift annuity comes with obligations.

59

When the charity receives the gift, it agrees to pay the donor a certain amount of money each year for as long as the donor lives (or for as long as the person or two people the donor designates will live). So, the charity doesn't have full use of the money at the time of the gift. Some states even require the charity to keep the money in a separate account. All of this recognizes the charity's duty to pay the donor each year for life.

The lifetime income stream for the donor also affects the donor. If the donor gave $10,000 cash as an outright gift, the income tax deduction would be $10,000. Pretty simple. But with a gift annuity, the donor is giving something less. While the donor is still giving the $10,000, the donor also receives something back: a promise of lifetime payments from the charity. That has a value that means the donor has really given something less than $10,000.

The donor's income tax deduction is reduced because of the addition of the life income stream into the donation equation. But reduced by how much?

The right to receive set payments for life has a value, and it is that value that is taken away from the income tax deduction. So with a gift annuity, the income tax deduction is never for the full amount. The IRS calculates the present value of the income stream and reduces the deduction accordingly.

Since gift annuities are designed for about half of the original funding amount to remain when the donor dies, the tax deduction, not surprisingly, usually comes out to be a little less than half of the funding amount.

With a gift annuity, each side gives something. Each side gets something. That's the split interest, and that's the beauty of the gift annuity. As we'll see in later chapters, the gift annuity is only one of several split interest gifts. It just happens to be the easiest to understand and the most common.

Gift Annuities are not Insurance

Although commonly confused for insurance, a gift annuity is not insurance, nor is it strictly a financial vehicle. It is only an agreement where the charity will pay the donor a set sum of money each year for as long as the donor lives. The amount of the payment is based on the amount of the donation and the donor's age when the donation is made.

To understand what a charitable gifting annuity is, it is important to understand what it is not. Many financial professionals believe the charitable gift annuity is some type of insurance. After all, a commercial annuity is a type of insurance product, so when you hear the words "charitable gift annuity," it is easy to see the misunderstanding.

Why is this distinction important? Many state regulations require you to make it clear to the donor that this is not insurance, nor is it guaranteed by anything or anyone other than the assets of the charity. In legal terms, a gift annuitant (the person receiving payments from the charity) is an unsecured creditor of the charity. In practical terms, the gift annuity is good only as long as the charity is around and able to make the payments.

But there is a second, vital reason, to distinguish between the contractual nature of gift annuities and the commercial worlds of insurance and finance. Because only nonprofits can issue gift annuities, many of our brethren in that commercial world will not like them. They will try to compete with you for the donor's "business."

As a good gift planner you will always advise your donors to check with their financial professionals and attorney before making any decision on a charitable gift annuity (or any significant donation to charity). If a donor goes to an unscrupulous professional or one who is starving for business, when the donor transfers money or assets from a brokerage account and gives it to you, that money comes not only from the donor, but also right from the bottom line of the financial professional!

In a sense, when someone takes money from a brokerage account to give to you, two donations are made: one from the donor and one from the professional that is losing the money from the managed account. For that reason, some brokers will often advise the donor to consider a commercial product that will remain under the broker's management. It will likely have, or appear to have, a higher payment rate or return for the donor, but will not have the tax benefits or charitable result your gift annuity will.

I don't mean to hover too long on the distinction between broker and gift officer, but too often, far too often, I have worked for a long time with a donor, running several illustrations over months of work only to discover that the broker re-advised the donor at the last minute to try a commercial product. It can be justified by the broker by saying the donor can always give the "extra money" earned to charity, based on how well the investment will perform.

While it is never our place to contradict the advice of the donor's professionals, it is our duty to educate the donor and ensure the donor knows exactly what a gift annuity is, how it benefits the donor, and how it differs from other vehicles, including commercial products with similar sounding names. Since the goal of this book is to help you establish more charitable gifts, it is important to point out areas where you might run into people who do not always share the same philanthropic goals.

People who can Help You with Gift Annuities

The first thing you should know is that no one completes a gift annuity alone. You either purchase (or your financial institution provides) you with gift annuity calculation software. A couple of decades ago, each gift annuity was a complex calculation involving pages of hand-figured numbers. Today, it is automated and easier.

There are two primary companies that make software to calculate and illustrate gift annuities: Crescendo Interactive, of Camarillo California, and PG Calc of Cambridge Massachusetts. I urge you to sample each company's software products to see which is right for you. Although the numbers should work out the same no matter which you use; the style, look and feel of each is different. It's a matter of comfort in how you feel about the user-friendliness of the software, and how well you perceive the support to be.

In addition to the gift annuity illustrations, their software packages include illustrations, contextual help and explanations for numerous planned gifts. Even better, they provide support and ongoing training. In planned giving, you are never alone, and fortunately, there are some good folks out there waiting to help you. Any gift annuity begins with the software that will do all the calculations for you.

Practical Steps to
Complete a Gift Annuity

Avoid using terms like *insurance* or *guaranty,* when describing charitable gift annuities. Those are words that belong to the commercial products of for-profit industries. Gift annuities are not insurance and are not guaranteed, as some financial instruments might be. They are a contract, and only a contract between the donor and charity.

Only nonprofits can issue charitable gift annuities. You, as a charity, have a monopoly. Market your organization and operate it knowing this reality. Learn everything you can about them and share that knowledge with donors.

- Let's say a donor wants to fund a gift annuity with you for $100,000. Here's what happens. You provide an illustration and sample contract for the donor, showing the payment rate, income tax deduction and other important facts about the gift annuity. An illustration is about six to sixteen pages, showing the details about the gift annuity. It illustrates the details and usually includes text definitions, charts, explanations and graphs. It is not, as the name might imply, a drawing. If you want to see one, call Crescendo Interactive or PG Calc (or both) and ask them to send you a sample illustration. They will be happy to supply you with one.

- If the donor likes the illustration, then you enter into a contract once the donor has given you the $100,000. The contract is usually only two or three pages.

- Although gift annuities are calculated based on annual payouts, you can choose to offer annual payments, each half-year, each quarter or each month. The most common payment is quarterly. Your gift annuity software will calculate these numbers for you.

Next, let your charity's finance office know that a gift annuity is about to begin. When the check or asset arrives, you work with your finance office to deposit the check or liquidate the asset and set up the donor's payment stream and prepare for tax documentation at the end of the year.

Let Someone Else do the Work for You

You may want to consider hiring a professional gift annuity management firm. Ask around. There are plenty of national companies that offer excellent service for surprisingly low fees. Either way, you need to make sure the funds are invested properly, and that you and your charity follow state law regulating investments and accounting (a good reason to hire a professional management firm).

You'll need to make sure you are prepared to make the payments accurately and on time for the rest of the donor's life. A good thing about hiring a professional management firm is they will often offer free or reduced-price training to improve your gift annuity marketing and management skills. So too, will your software provider.

You may consider reinsuring your organization's gift annuities. Large insurance companies will manage your gift annuity program for you. You pay for the service, but if your organization wants to minimize risk, reinsurance is worth exploring.

Let the Benefits Begin

As soon as the contract is signed and funds received, the donor has made a gift that is eligible for treatment as an income tax deduction. This deduction is for the *current year*. The donor's income tax deduction is for about one half of the funding amount. That "half" (actually closer to 40-45 percent), represents the money the donor will not get back, or the present value of the expected payment stream as discussed earlier.

Whether the donor lives only a day after funding the gift annuity, or lives twenty years beyond the donor's predicted lifespan, the payments continue at the same amount every year for life. It is your responsibility to wisely invest these funds and keep track of gift annuities so that your investments maintain the principal value and hopefully grow even as payments are made.

Because the income tax deduction is immediate, it never changes. However, if the donor cannot use all of it in the current year, the donor can carry it forward up to five years, using as much of it as possible each year, until exhausted.

When the gift annuity beneficiary or beneficiaries die, money left in the gift annuity goes directly to your nonprofit. As with any other gift, the donor can restrict the gift or designate according to the policies and needs of your organization.

Parties Involved with Each Gift Annuity

There are at least five "parties" with each gift annuity:

- The donor,

- your organization,

- the American Council on Gift Annuities (ACGA), which sets the payment rates you will follow,

- the state where your organization is based and the state where the donor lives,

- your software vendor (Crescendo Interactive or PGCalc) providing the program generating the illustration and possibly the gift annuity contract for you.

Reinsurance

Reinsurance is a way of minimizing risk. You transfer the responsibility for payments to another organization, usually a large insurance company. They handle the checks or direct deposit and tax forms. However, your organization is never "off the hook." You just have a partner on the hook with you.

The downside is you pay for that service, sometimes significantly. You also might lose a little marketing opportunity too, because there is value in having the checks come from you and not from an insurance company reinsurer. Checks received with your charity's imprint and logo help strengthen the relationship between donor and charity. That is always a good thing and often results in more gift annuities, so weigh all sides when deciding on whether to reinsure.

Don't be Intimidated

On my first day working for one charity, my assistant walked in with a pile of checks and said I needed to mail them to donors. I was confused. *Don't donors mail us checks*? I happened to start on the day gift annuity checks were to go out – and I had no idea what a gift annuity was and no idea what to do with the checks. They assumed I did because I was an attorney.

I quickly read up on gift annuities. More than fourteen years later I still learn something every day about charitable giving. It is always okay to ask questions, and I have tried to point out areas in this book where even "experts" hold onto misbeliefs when they should know better. So at the starting point, I am helping you perform better than people who have done this for years. Hopefully, you won't have to experience some of the surprises I found when I started in planned giving.

Donors and Charitable Organizations

We've already talked about the donor's benefits and the charity's obligations and the remainder interest, but what about the American Council on Gift Annuities, the states, and the vendors?

The American Council on Gift Annuities

The American Council on Gift Annuities is a nonprofit organization. It was formed in 1927 to help charities learn about and promote charitable gift annuities. One of its primary roles is to hire actuaries and accountants to publish one-life and two-life gift annuity rates. The nonprofit board and its advisors watch for changes in the economy and in laws governing gift annuities and they update the rates from time to time.

Before there was Order there was Chaos

Early in the history of gift annuities, charities set their own payment rates. Charities were competing for donors based on those rates. Today, one of the most important roles of the Council is to standardize rates.

Most charities follow ACGA rates. That way donors fund gift annuities with nonprofits based on their affinity with the charity and its mission. Rather than compete or enter bidding wars for a donor's money, with few exceptions, charities all offer the same payment rates.

Occasionally a donor will call asking if you can beat another nonprofit's payment rate. Resist the temptation to increase your rate, even a little, over ACGA rates. You'll save yourself a lot of trouble and headache.

Do yourself and all of us a favor and follow the ACGA rates. The rates are based on sound financial calculations, and besides, we all want to live in a world where donors choose us on mission and not payment rates. You can learn more about gift annuities and the ACGA at its website: acga-web.org.

Check out the American Council on Gift Annuities' website. But remember, its address is acga-web.org. If you go to acga.org you'll find another ACGA, the American Corn Growers Association website.

When the ACGA does change rates, it does not affect the rates of existing contracts. It only changes the rates for contracts formed after the new rates take effect. Most charities in this country follow the ACGA rates. A few follow the rates but cap them at a certain level or choose to be even more conservative.

A handful of charities set their own rates, or choose to routinely offer rates higher or more aggressive than ACGA rates. The first word in charitable gift annuity is "charitable." A donor should fund one with charitable intent, not because of aggressive marketing or for the income it will provide.

Gift annuities are first and foremost a gift to your cause or mission. While you should actively market and point out the attractive payment rates and tax benefits, they are second to the donor's desire for their money to benefit your organization's mission.

The States

Each of our 50 states has the option of regulating gift annuities. Some do. Some don't. Some that do, regulate them heavily. Some that do, regulate them only a little. It is critical that if you offer gift annuities, you comply with federal law, state law and follow rates established by the ACGA.

Unless you are a gift annuity expert, find someone who is, or hire someone to guide you through the state regulation process. If you are new to gift annuities, this is not an area where you can self-educate. Crescendo Interactive, PG Calc and other vendors offer registration services.

Use one of them or contact your investment advisor for gift annuity compliance information. Take advantage of these experts to help you complete your registration.

Anyone can claim to register you for gift annuities with the state authorities. Beware of those who do this work only occasionally, or try their hand at it with you for the first time. They may charge ten times as much as organizations that register gift annuities routinely. Check around. You can save a lot of time and money, not to mention frustration! Begin by asking your planned giving software provider what it charges to register your organization in your state and the states where your donors live.

While it can sound intimidating when you talk about regulation and all the finer points that go into gift annuities, it need not be. Use this book as a starting point and as a guide to find the right experts and partners to make your gift annuities a success.

I have funded hundreds of gift annuities over the years and served as a consultant and investment provider, managing hundreds of gift annuities for other charities. It is still thrilling when a gift annuity contract is signed. The charity is happy to receive the donation and the donor is happy to give it.

Gift Annuity Varieties
You Can Offer Your Donor

There are two things all gift annuities have in common:

- Payment rates are always based on the age or ages of the beneficiaries.

- Gift annuities can only be for one or two *lives*, never more and never less (corporations cannot fund a gift annuity).

After that however, there are several options. Here are some varieties and choices available for your donors to consider.

One-Life Gift Annuity

This is the most common gift annuity. While the donor is more commonly the beneficiary as well, it is possible for the donor to fund a gift annuity for someone else, naming him or her as beneficiary.

Two-Life Gift Annuities

Similar to the one-life gift annuity, donors can fund one for himself or herself and another person, or fund it as a gift for two others. There are special rates for two-life gift annuities since there is a greater life expectancy, therefore payment duration, for two people than there is for one.

Remember that as with all gift annuities, the payment rates are based on the beneficiaries' ages and not the donor's age. The most common two-life gift annuity is funded by a husband and wife, with payments to them for as long as either lives.

Deferred Gift Annuities

A donor can get a higher rate by waiting a few years for the first payment. You and the donor agree to the date of the first payment. The longer the wait, the higher the payment, *and* the higher the income tax deduction.

If the donor dies between the time of funding and the date of the first payment, all of the money goes directly to the charity. That's the risk that goes with the reward of higher payments and higher tax deductions. Deferred gift annuities can be used with one life or two life gift annuities.

Even More Options for Gift Annuities?

A *college annuity* defers payments for a number of years, pays for four years and then stops. A *flexible deferred gift annuity* allows the donor to wait for the first payment, achieving the higher payment rate of a deferred gift annuity, but also gives the donor the flexibility to later choose to wait even longer for the first payment, getting an even higher rate.

The college and flexible deferred gift annuity are rare. Just know they're out there, and once you feel comfortable with regular, run-of-the-mill gift annuities, start exploring and learning the many options you can offer donors.

The Many Ways of Funding Gift Annuities

Donors can fund a gift annuity in one of three ways:

- Cash (the most popular option)

- Appreciated assets (such as stock)

- Property (usually real estate, but could be personal property like jewelry or a plane).

Gift Annuities and Capital Gains from Stock

Funding a gift annuity with stock is an excellent idea. Remember capital gains from Chapter Two? If a donor sells stock, the donor pays a capital gains tax on the appreciation of that stock. This is true even if the donor gives the cash from the sale to charity a moment later.

Using a gift of stock, it is crucial that the donor **never sell** the stock. The donor must hand your charity the paper shares or have them directly transferred electronically to your charity's brokerage account. The value of the stock is calculated as the average of the high and low selling price on the day the stock enters your account. It is irrelevant what the charity may receive when it later sells the stock, or what it is worth when the stock enters the charity's account.

When a donor funds a gift annuity with stock, a portion of the capital gains tax is *eliminated*. This is the portion attributed to the expected "gift" portion of the annuity (this goes back to the "split-interest" concept we learned earlier). The remaining capital gains are spread equally over the expected lifespan of the donor. Put another way, a portion of each stock gift is calculated to be invested and used to pay back the donor. The other portion is calculated to be left over for the charity at the donor's death.

If the donor funds a gift annuity for someone else using appreciated assets, then all of the capital gains tax is payable at the time of funding. If you are dealing with appreciated assets be sure to find a mentor and check with him or her as you go along, at least for the first couple of annuities like this. Your illustration software will also help you with gifts of stock.

Taxation of Payments to the Donor

When the gift annuity payments come to the donor, the government considers the payments in different ways for tax purposes. Remembering that a gift annuity is a split-interest gift, meaning the donor gives something to charity and also gets something back, the way the payments are taxed reflects this split approach.

With each payment the donor receives by check (or direct deposit) the government considers that payment to be made of up to three parts:

- Return of principal (tax-free to donor)

- Income (taxed at donor's income tax rate)

- Capital gains (if the gift annuity was funded with an appreciated asset, which is taxed at the donor's capital gains tax rate)

Some of the money is simply a return of the donor's original funding amount, the principal. The government also assumes the charity is investing the donor's money and some of each payment is from the fruits of that investment (whether it actually is or not). Finally, if the donor used an appreciated asset like stock to fund the gift, the government assumes that some of each payment represents the donor's gain in the stock.

If donors live beyond their expected lifespans (as calculated at the formation of the gift), the taxation switches. The donor is now in bonus time! The government assumes the donor has "used up," all of the principal—it has all been returned, and the donor has already paid all the gains on any appreciated asset. Now the charity is paying the donor from the income it has made or should have made on the investment of the donation, *or from its operating funds*. So the donor pays ordinary income tax on all subsequent payments.

When you give your donor a gift annuity illustration, it calculates the taxation for the next twenty or thirty years or more. Donors will see—and ask—why the taxation of the payments change at a certain point. Now you know. That point is the year they are expected to die (according to mortality tables) and the taxing characteristics change when the donor lives beyond this date. And, while it is seldom seen as worth mentioning to a donor, if a donor dies prior to the actuary's calculation, the donor's estate can take advantage of the unused capital gain if stocks were used to fund the gift.

The Applicable Federal Rate
One Last Technical Detail

Another variable in gift annuities is the Applicable Federal Rate (AFR). When using software to illustrate a gift annuity, you will be asked what AFR you want to use.

Choose Wisely

The AFR is a barometer on the US economy. The United States Treasury publishes this rate every month. This rate enters into the calculations of the taxes on the gift annuity.

A higher AFR gives a donor a larger income tax deduction this year, but a slightly larger portion of each payment will be taxed as income. The upshot of the AFR is that the donor can get a slightly better tax treatment in the year of the gift or take that same benefit spread out over the donor's expected lifespan.

The reasoning is simple. A higher AFR means the donor could keep the money and invest it to get a higher return. The converse is true for low AFRs, too.

With gift annuities, the donor can choose from the AFR rate of the month of the gift, or from the prior two months. For example, if the donor makes a gift annuity on May 15, the donor can choose May's AFR or choose the one from April or March. Your software program allows your donor to pick appropriately. Just make sure you have updated the rates (usually automatically) in your software and have chosen the correct gift date.

The important thing to remember is that you must always let the donor choose the AFR that's right for the donor. The theory is the federal government doesn't want donors to rush into a gift annuity or try to time the funding. So donors always have the choice of using the AFR for the current month or for the prior two months. Sometimes the economy isn't changing much and all three months have the same rate.

The AFR choice rarely changes the balances very much, but it is nice to show the donor a choice and let the donor choose which benefits are most important to the donor. In my experience, most donors choose the higher immediate income tax deduction when funding the gift, but it is mandatory that the donor choose, so let each donor know the options.

The Reasoning Behind the Rates

Your donor may ask where the rates come from and what they mean. After explaining about the ACGA, you can also explain what the ACGA uses to come up with them.

The full explanation is on the ACGA's website (acga-web.org) under the "about the rates" tab.

Some of the variables change, but in essence the formula the ACGA uses to calculate rates is the following:

- The ACGA bases the calculations on a target of 50 percent residuum, or that half of the funding amount will be left over for the charity if the donor lives the expected lifespan. The lifespan is based upon the Annuity 2000 Mortality Tables. The rates also incorporate projections for increasing life expectancies (improvements in mortality) using a scale supplied by the ACGA's actuary.

- The present value of the residuum must be at least 20 percent of the original contribution for the annuity.

- All annuitants are assumed to be women and one year younger than their actual ages.

- The rates assume the charity will have annual investment and administrative expenses of 1 percent of the Fair Market Value of gift annuity reserves.

- As of the date of this book's publication, the ACGA bases rates on a gross actual investment return of 4.25 percent. The ACGA adjusts this number when the economy warrants.

More Reasoning Behind the Rates

For a gift annuity to be valid, the federal government requires that the charitable deduction must be calculated to be at least 10 percent of the original funding amount at the time of funding.

Gift Annuities and the Philanthropy Protection Act

In 1995, Congress passed a law that relates to charitable gift annuities. It requires certain information to be included in gift annuity contracts (essentially making clear the relationship between charity and donor) and also regulates how gift annuities may be issued.

Language and regulations change. Before soliciting a gift annuity, check the ACGA website and check with your software vendor to make sure you comply. Work with your charity's counsel to make sure your disclosure statement and program are in compliance and up-to-date.

Use appropriate disclosure language when first discussing charitable gift annuities with a donor and use proper language in your contracts. Importantly, the ACGA and software providers provide a sample disclosure letter and appropriate language in their contracts.

Marketing Gift Annuities

To help you get the word out on gift annuities, here are some ideas.

- Ask your gift annuity software provider for marketing samples and ideas.

- Ask your gift annuity software provider to point you to some charities "doing it rightly," so you can follow their example. There is nothing wrong with learning from the best – and from being on their mailing list.

- Look out for your donors by letting them know when their rates are going up, or about to go down (if they are considering funding one, or another one).

- Use the words "dependable," "reliable," and "fixed," when communicating about gift annuities.

- Do not use the words "guaranty," or "insure," since they are not related to gift annuities.

- Ask your existing annuitants why they chose to fund their gift annuities, then market to others accordingly.

- Compare your gift annuities to current CD rates and the attractiveness of fixed rates, helping your mission, and the tax benefits.

In summary, use your imagination, but remember to under-promise and over-deliver. Gift annuities are wonderful vehicles that don't need to be "sold." You need only make donors aware of their availability and their benefits.

A Little Trivia

For calculations, the ACGA considers all annuitants to be women. Women live longer than men, so even if a husband and wife fund a gift annuity together, the ACGA considers both to be women, just to be a little more conservative. If you assume donors will live a little longer when calculating the cost of a lifetime of payments, you are safer in calculating what you promise to pay.

A Little More Trivia

The IRS rounds up your birthday. When we are within six months of our next birthday, the IRS considers us to already be there! If you have a donor who turns 87 in four months, he gets the rate as if he was already 87 years old. There are many marketing opportunities when you keep your donors' birthdays in mind.

The Beauty of a Gift Annuity

Although gift annuities can sound a little complicated, they really are not. Just know that gift annuities are their own breed of gift and as such require a little extra attention. However, that little extra effort goes a long way.

Because there is nothing else quite like gift annuities, they are especially attractive to donors. Donors love them. Explore gift annuities; look at websites like acga-web.org, pgcalc.com and crescendointeractive.com for lots of good information and ideas.

To Recap:

- Gift annuities are a contract between a charity and a donor, where the charity agrees to pay the donor a fixed payment for life, based on the amount contributed and the age of the beneficiaries.

- Gift annuities are not insurance.

- Gift annuities are regulated by the states and federal government and it is important to comply with these laws.

- Only nonprofit organizations can issue gift annuities.

- Gift annuities offer income tax and estate tax benefits, and when funded with transfers of stock, capital gains tax benefits.

- Gift annuities can be for one or two people and can be offered with several options such as deferring the first payment to receive a higher payment rate.

Chapter 5   Trusts

The Power of Possibilities

- Trust Me, Trusts are Terrific
  - How Trusts Work
  - Why Donors Trust Trusts

The Power of Trusts

Trusts can be a wonderful, although often overlooked, tool for helping the right donor make a spectacular gift to charity. Unfortunately, while trusts can be used in different ways and offer a multitude of features to be mixed and matched to meet a donor's particular goals, they are not used as much as they can, or perhaps, should be.

In the same way you do not need to know engine maintenance and repair to drive your car to work, I am not going to cover every detail about trusts; just enough to expose you to wonderful opportunities while warning you of possible dangers and traps. In the same way driving school teaches you about tire pressure, oil changes and basic maintenance, but not how to rebuild a carburetor, we'll look at the basics of what makes trusts tick.

The Importance of Independent Counsel

When dealing with trusts, always encourage your donors to rely on professionals who work with these instruments daily. Aside from the fact that training, practice and experience count; laws change frequently and sometimes dramatically. Besides, only the donor's professional advisor knows aspects of the donor's situation we are simply not privy to know.

No matter how skilled one might be in estate planning, you cannot represent a charity and draft a will or trust for a donor; nor can anyone representing you as a staff member or volunteer. It is a conflict of interest for the entity benefiting from the gift to draft it for the donor. This is yet another reason for the donor to have independent counsel and advice.

Trusts – How they Began
is Still Important Today

I want to give you a gift that was never given to me. Most trust training, especially as it relates to charitable giving, begins at the end. Whether it's on-the-job training, school of hard knocks, or through formalized course work, most trust education focuses on the types of trusts and under which situations each is most advantageous.

Why not begin at the beginning? It is far more effective, but far less utilized, to start at the beginning and walk through it. If we can look at how trusts began, it is much easier to see why they behave the way they do today.

What Exactly is a Trust Anyway?

Trusts have been around a long time. Thousands of years. Maybe since the beginning of time. They probably took on the name "trust," in England 500 or so years ago.

Trusts are mentioned several times in the Bible, and in other ancient texts. There are many Biblical parables about the master, usually a farmer, going on a journey, and asking the servants or family to watch the farm while he is gone.

He left the property in what we would now call "trust." A trust is really no more complicated than that. That is, at least, until we start asking the trust to do complicated things!

Parties to a Trust

At its essence, a trust has three parties:

- The donor or property owner (in the parable above, the farmer)

- The trustee (the person the donor designates to make decisions for the property in his absence–whether literal or figurative)

- The beneficiary (in the parable above, the beneficiary is also the donor. But as we will see, the beneficiary of a charitable trust is a charity, hopefully *yours*).

Modern trusts are governed by written agreements. They are binding on the trustee to do what the donor wants to be done with the donor's property. The trust also dictates who gets income from the trust, who can take from the trust's principal assets, and who gets whatever's left in the trust when the trust terminates.

Back to Trust History

Modern trust law started in Great Britain as it emerged from the Middle Ages. Landowners, the privileged class in England, would leave to conduct business.

They could be gone months or years. As they were about to leave, it is easy for us to visualize them sitting down with a trusted tenant or servant, detailing what is supposed to be done with the land and farm while he was gone. They created a trust.

As the servant waived goodbye, he now became the master of the land; making decisions as if he were the owner, on behalf of the owner, following the owner's instructions. The servant became the trustee. People in the village could deal with the trustee as if he were the landowner and could count on his decisions as binding on the owner and the land.

The problem was that sometimes the landowner never came home. Sometimes the landowner would return to find the servant had not followed orders. Or occasionally, the lord of the land (do you see where we get the term "landlord?") would find his home had been greatly improved by the tenant and everyone around the village had forgotten who the landlord even was!

With increasing regularity, landlords would take their servants to court (the "Crown") for assistance. This is where trust law bumps into another maxim we all know: "possession is 9/10 of the law." Often the courts would side with the tenant. After all, the landlord was away doing whatever he wanted to do, while the poor servants at home poured their hearts and souls into the land and improved it as if it were theirs. Sometimes so much so, it *became* theirs.

The privileged class did not like such court decisions.

The Beginning of Modern Trust Law

England began enacting laws to govern trusts. The most important rule was that all trusts had to be in writing. With written agreements, it would be easier to see who had responsibility for what actions. The trust could account for contingencies at the outset so the parties would have a mutual understanding as to what would happen to the property.

The early laws that governed English trusts hundreds of years ago are still pretty much with us today. Trusts also continue to be the source of court decisions and the subject of new laws every year.

So why learn about trust history, if all we want to do is guide gifts to our mission? Because if you think of trusts as a *relationship* more than as a form you download from the computer, you are ahead of most charities and gift officers.

You will be able to better serve your donors over people who attempt to push the donor into one planned giving vehicle over another. When a donor has better choices, your organization is more likely to be named as a beneficiary.

Modern Trusts

Today, there are many types of trusts. Only a fraction are specifically designed for charitable purposes. When we discuss trusts, we will only be concerned with charitable trusts and with living trusts with charitable intent.

The modern trust relationship (in the charitable context) has three parties.

- Donor– the person or family with an asset to place under the ownership of a trust.

- Trustee– the person or corporation that will have legal authority to control the asset while it is under the trust. The trustee's authority and liability are spelled out in the trust agreement and controlled by state law. National, or federal laws may also come into play.

- Beneficiary– the person or entity who will receive some or all of the trust assets either during the life of the trust or when the trust terminates.

A trust can have multiple donors, multiple trustees and multiple beneficiaries. It should also specify successor trustees and successor beneficiaries to take the place of the primary ones, if the need arises.

Sometimes the donor is also a beneficiary. A donor can also act as trustee. Remember: trusts are full of possibilities. However, each state has specific laws governing trusts. Sometimes the rules make clear sense. Sometimes they may not seem to make sense, at least on the surface.

Most planned giving officers, and certainly most charities, when working with a donor, jump right to the most complex types of trusts when talking with donors. All the options, bells, whistles, and tax advantages of CRUTs, CRATs, and NIMCRUTs (these are all names of types of trusts) are especially enticing to explain and illustrate. However, the amount of money in charitable trusts in this country pales compared to the amount of money in living trusts.

Encourage your donor to get independent legal advice about trusts, and you do the same. But it is a bonus, and the purpose of this book, when you can arm your donor with specific questions to ask counsel. For example, "Ask your attorney about the benefits of placing your highly appreciated stock in a charitable remainder unitrust. Here are some ideas to ask why this might or might not be a good idea."

Want to see how many people have charitable trusts in this country and some other interesting statistics? Go to irs.gov and do a search for charitable remainder trust statistics (or split interest trust statistics). It will give you a great snapshot of split-interest trusts (charitable trusts).

Living and Testamentary Trusts

A living trust is a trust that is created while someone is alive. People fund living trusts all the time. A living trust differs from a testamentary trust, which begins when the person dies. Testamentary trusts are generally created in a person's will.

A donor can leave (or designate) money to charity in a living trust or in a testamentary trust. This is a common source of charitable donations. They just lack some of the specific tax benefits and payment options of charitable remainder trusts.

We often use the word "estate planning," when we talk about wills. Wills are certainly part of an estate plan, but trusts are equally important to proper planning. When a donor tells you your charity is a beneficiary of a trust, that is good news, if not better news, than being named a beneficiary of a will. Studies by Professor Russell James at Texas Tech University indicate a donor is more likely to preserve a gift to a trust beneficiary than to a will beneficiary[1].

How Long Do Trusts Last?

Trusts can be designed to last three ways:

- For a term of years.

- For the duration of someone's life, or for the lives of several people.

- Or for a combination of a term of years and a life or lives.

When a trust donor wants to benefit family members, a common method is a trust with a duration measured by lives. The trust exists based on the "lives" of real people, as in: "this trust will continue for as long as Johnny, Mary, or Susie lives."

Notably, and interestingly, the lives used to measure the trust do not have to be beneficiaries of the trust. You can set up a trust to terminate ten years after the last of Johnny, Mary, and Susie to die. There are many variables and combinations of variables available to the donor.

---

[1] Please see this and other great research and tips at www.encouragegenerosity.com

A term of years trust is fairly simple. It lasts as long as the donor designates; limited only by state laws and the longevity of the assets administered by the trust.

A term of years trust looks like this:
"This trust shall last seven years."
A life trust might read, "For as long as Donor
or Donor's Wife lives."

As with wills, unless required by state law, no charity has to be notified that it is a remainder beneficiary of a trust.

Charitable Trusts

Charitable trusts are trusts that meet special requirements as established by Congress and regulated by the IRS. If an attorney follows the rules when setting up a charitable trust, your donor will have some tax benefits that living and testamentary trusts do not offer.

One of the first benefits is the avoidance of estate taxes. When a donor places an asset into a charitable trust (either a remainder or lead trust) those assets are not going to be part of the donor's estate. This is helpful for high net worth donors who might be subject to the estate tax.

Estate taxes, also known as death taxes, can extract a huge toll on what a donor leaves behind. Avoiding or reducing their impact is not inconsequential. Avoiding or reducing the estate tax is only one of many benefits of a charitable trust.

There are two broad categories of charitable trusts:

- Charitable Remainder Trust

- Charitable Lead Trust

Here is a brief comparison of the two trusts and what each is more commonly used for:

Trust	During the life of the trust	At the end of the trust	Is excellent for
Charitable Remainder Trust	Payments go to person or people designated by donor.	Remaining funds in the trust transfer to charity.	Tax-wise giving, income for the donor, and a sizeable charitable gift.
Charitable Lead Trust	Payments go to charity.	Remainder goes to the donor or donor's family.	Immediate cash for charity and an opportunity to lessen generation skipping taxes.

The two are alike in that trust assets have been irrevocably pledged to a charitable beneficiary (or beneficiaries). The donor or the person setting up the trust has promised that money from the trust will go to a nonprofit (qualified charity).

In the charitable remainder trust, which is more common, the trust pays the donor money during the life of the trust and then the remainder goes to charity.

With a lead trust, the trust pays money to a charity during the life of the trust and then the remainder goes back to the donor or the donor's family.

In all cases the amount of money in the trust varies with how the money is invested and how it is paid out. It will also vary with the length of the trust, how many beneficiaries there are, and what types of assets the trust holds.

For both the charitable remainder trust and charitable lead trust there are charitable and non-charitable beneficiaries. The non-charitable beneficiaries are usually the donor or donor's family, or perhaps the donor's grandchildren.

A simple way of remembering these is that a "charitable remainder trust" is so named because a charity gets the remainder. A charitable lead trust has the charity getting the money in the lead (at first).

Now let's look more specifically at how they differ.

Charitable Remainder Trusts

Congress created and the IRS recognizes the concept of a charitable remainder trust, or charitable remainder unitrust. Both terms describe the same entity and you will hear both terms used interchangeably. Sometimes people just call it a "unitrust."

While the regulations and cases interpreting charitable remainder trusts could fill volumes and occupy law school professors' careers, the distinguishing feature to remember is that a charitable remainder trust names a charity (as recognized by the IRS) as *remainder* beneficiary. In more common terms, when the trust terminates, some or all of anything left over will go to charity or charities.

Charitable Remainder Unitrust Example

Fred is 80 years old. He creates a charitable remainder trust that will last for his lifetime. During his life, the trust will pay him 5 percent of trust assets (Later, we will look at how the 5 percent is calculated). He names ABC Charity, a local nonprofit food bank, as the remainder beneficiary.

Fred gets money each year for as long as he lives (or until the trust runs out of money), and when he dies the charity receives the remainder. How much is left depends on how long he lives and how the funds are invested.

Did you notice who got to name this kind of trust? Charities, that's who! If donors had named it they would have called it a "Family First Trust," because in practice, that's what it is. It is usually family members who receive the benefits of the trust for a time and the charity gets the leftovers. Apparently, charities had a strong political lobby and this is one time when we describe the meal as what's left in the doggy bag and not what was originally on the table!

How Does a Remainder Trust Pay Each Year?

In the example above, Fred specified that 5 percent of the trust would be paid to him each year for the life of the trust. Each year, the trustee must measure the value of the trust and pay 5 percent of whatever that value is.

The trustee also has a duty to follow the instructions of the trust document and to invest the money prudently. If the trust investments do well, that means Fred gets more. The 5 percent is based on trust assets as measured on December 31 of the year that just ended.

If the trust grows faster than the outgoing payments, Fred gets more money each year that growth happens. Five percent of $100 is $5. Five percent of $110 is $5.50. There will be more than the original funding amount left over for the charity, assuming the investment return continues to be higher than the payments.

When the donor chooses a payout rate, there must be a balance between anticipated trust growth and payouts. Too high a payout results in the trust diminishing too quickly. This means less money for the donor and ultimately less money for the charity.

As the donor sets the payment rate higher, the income tax deduction also goes down, because less money is calculated to be left for the charity. A very low payment rate lets the trust grow faster and leaves more for the charity. A low payment rate is not all bad for the donor. Remember, that since the donor receives a percentage of the trust, as the trust grows, so do the payments to the donor.

In addition to valuing the trust at least annually, and in addition to making payments, the trustee must also make sure proper tax returns are filed with the IRS. The IRS assigns a taxpayer identification number (TIN) to the trust and just like an individual or a corporation, the trustee must report to the IRS each year.

Greater than Five
Less than Fifty

When choosing a payment rate, the Tax Code also adds some guardrails. The Code mandates that the payout rate must be 5 percent or greater, but less than or equal to 50 percent. The Code also states that based on the trust terms, the present value of the charitable remainder interest at funding must be at least equal to 10 percent.

Whether you are the life beneficiary or charity, you want the trust investments to perform well during the early years of the trust. That way the trust's value has an opportunity to grow.

If a trust performs poorly in its first year, you suffer a double whammy. Not only is the original trust amount down, but now it will be down another 5 percent or whatever the payment rate is.

And as any investor or mathematician will tell you, even if the trust does well the next year, there is less money to invest and the road back to prosperity is clearly uphill. Keep this in mind as we consider other types of charitable trusts.

Tax Benefits of Unitrusts

Because the trust is calculated to have money remaining for the charity, and the formulas for payments are set when funding the trust, the donor receives an income tax deduction in the year the trust is created. When calculating the donor's income tax deduction for funding a charitable remainder trust, there are several factors:

- The life expectancy of the trust: For a life trust, it is based on standard mortality tables and the lives of the people on which the trust is based. Of course, a term of years trust is easier to measure. It's just the number of years designated by the trust.

- The payment rate: The higher the payment rate during the life of the trust, the less that will be left over for the charity. The higher the payment rate, the lower the deduction will be.

- The economy: The IRS provides an Applicable Federal Rate, which is the same rate we discussed in the chapter on gift annuities. The AFR acts as a barometer of the economy. A higher AFR chosen by the donor means a higher income tax deduction today, and slightly more taxation of the yearly payments. A lower AFR produces a lower income tax deduction this year, but slightly more favorable taxation during the life of the trust.

As with gift annuities, the IRS looks at the trust at its formation to determine how much of an income tax deduction the donor receives in the year the trust is funded.

Capital Gains Benefits (When Using Stock to Fund a CRUT)

The benefits of a remainder trust increase considerably when the donor funds it using appreciated assets such as stock. Because the remainder trust is a qualified trust, the assets can be transferred to the trust (never sold) without the donor paying any capital gains tax. Accountants call this "bypassing" the capital gains. If the trust investments perform well enough that the trust corpus (the original trust funding amount) is never touched, then the capital gains are bypassed permanently. No capital gains tax is ever paid by the donor.

Even if the trust corpus is used or stocks within the trust are sold, and capital gain is realized in making payments to the donor, the payments are taxed at the capital gains rate, which is generally lower than the donor's income tax rates.

Taxation of Payments to Non-Charitable Beneficiaries

Since the trust is a charitable trust, it does not pay taxes. However, whenever the trustee makes payments to the non-charitable beneficiaries, those payments are subject to state and federal taxation for the beneficiaries.

The amount of taxes the income beneficiary or beneficiaries must pay is based on how the trustee invested the trust assets the year before. Essentially whatever the trust would have paid if it were a taxable trust is passed on directly to the income beneficiaries.

The trustee follows a four-tier rule when reporting income to the beneficiaries. The trustee must pay out trust income in the following order:

> 1. Ordinary Income—Income from interest and dividends. Just as it would be if you or I received interest or dividends, this income is taxed as ordinary income. Ordinary Income tax rates are generally the highest.

> 2. Long-Term Capital Gains—Proceeds resulting from the trust's sale of appreciated assets it has held one year or longer. Capital gains rates are generally lower, and more attractive than ordinary income tax rates.

> 3. Tax-Exempt Income—Income resulting from investments in tax-exempt institutions. This is generally municipal and other government bonds.

> 4. Return of Principal—A distribution from the trust's principal assets. A distribution of principal assets is not taxable to the beneficiary.

The Four-Tier Approach to Taxation

Corpus

Tax-Free

Capital Gains

Income

You will often hear the taxation of trusts compared to a bucket filled with four different liquids. The top "liquid" is "principal." The next liquid is tax-exempt income, followed by long-term capital gains. At the bottom is ordinary income.

The trustee controls the spigot at the bottom by turning it on to pay the beneficiaries the "liquids" from the bucket. Since the hole is at the bottom, the payments first come from ordinary income earned by the trust. Once that is used up, or if it never existed, the payments come from long-term capital gains, and so on.

While the trustee cannot change the order the government requires for tax purposes, the trustee can control the taxation by choosing the investments in such a way that the "bottom," (more taxingly painful assets) are minimized and the tax-favorable assets produce most of the payments.

The trustee, while bound to act prudently, meaning seeking a reasonable return, will invest in assets to maximize trust income and growth, while balancing the taxation of payments for the life beneficiaries.

A portfolio, for example, of only municipal bonds means the donors will never pay taxes on the payments. However, that rate of return might be unattractive compared to other investment opportunities. The trustee must balance a duty to invest prudently with a desire to limit taxes paid by the noncharitable beneficiaries.

Consider a $10,000 payment from a Charitable Remainder Unitrust to a life beneficiary. The trustee will provide the recipient with a breakdown of the source of the payment, which might look like this:

Interest	$4,000
Capital gains	$3,500
Tax-exempt income	$1,500
Return of principal	$1,000
Total	$10,000

The beneficiary would pay *income tax* on $4,000 and *capital gains tax* on $3,500 based on the beneficiary's capital gains rate. The donor enjoys the $1,500 and $1,000 from the tax-exempt income and return of principal portion without paying any taxes on that part of the distribution!

Variations of the Charitable Remainder Trust

Below are some variations of the charitable remainder trust that offer even more opportunities to make it work better for the donor. These decisions must be made at the formation of the trust and are reflected by the trust language itself. Once established, the character of a trust cannot be changed.

Charitable Remainder Annuity Trust

The CRAT, as it's known, is for a donor who likes predictability. Unlike a CRUT that pays out a percentage of trust assets, the CRAT pays out the same amount each year. That's where the word "annuity" comes from in the name. The trust's ability to make those payments is still dependent on the selection of a prudent payment amount, the predicted life of the trust and reasonable investment assumptions. But some donors like this option because they know exactly how much the trust will pay each year.

Net Income Unitrust

This unitrust is just like the standard unitrust, but with one exception. It pays the fixed percentage designated by the trust or the net income of the trust, *whichever is less*. Not a bad idea if your donor is more interested in preserving the trust corpus than getting high payments.

This generally presents a greater remainder for the charitable beneficiary than other types of remainder trusts as the principal is never reduced by payments. The only way it can be less is if the trustee invests in assets that lose value.

Net Income with Makeup Unitrust

Commonly called a NIMCRUT, it takes the Net Income Unitrust one step further. This trust pays the fixed percentage or actual income as the trust is revalued each year; *whichever is less*. However, with the "make-up" provision added to the trust, the trustee can use later years of excess income to "make-up" shortfalls in prior years.

This provision is especially handy when the donor uses property to fund the trust that is difficult to value or does not produce income early in the life of the trust. Such assets might be real estate, farmland, or closely held stock.

FLIP Unitrust

The FLIP Unitrust combines the advantages of several types of unitrusts to benefit donors in specific situations. It begins life as a net income trust, but typically generates no income for the first part of its life. Since there is no net income, it has nothing to distribute.

The FLIP Unitrust anticipates a specific event. After the event, the trust "flips" to become a regular unitrust. The event might be a life event, such as retirement or the sale of an asset that was placed in the trust. For example, if a donor contributes 500 acres of timber to the trust, but the timber is five years from maturity, it will not produce any income for five years.

Prudent investment rules do not force the trustee to harvest immature trees or sell off pieces of the land. However, in the fifth year of the trust, there should be a surge in income as the timber is harvested and sold.

The trustee can use that income to make up for the five previous years of little or no payments. There are some restrictions on the types of investments that might be made and how they are invested, so the donor is urged to check with counsel.

Charitable Lead Trusts

The lead trust is the complement to the CRUT. Where a CRUT gives benefits to family for life and to charity for the remainder, the lead trust provides the opposite.

The donor transfers assets to a trust; usually cash or publicly traded stock. This trust is designed for a term of years. During the life of the trust, it pays income to the charity. After, the remainder goes to those family members or friends specified by the donor in the trust.

Lead trusts are less common than remainder trusts. However, they are especially attractive to wealthy individuals wishing to pass significant sums to children, and especially to grandchildren. The charitable lead trust helps avoid estate, gift, and generation-skipping taxes, which would each otherwise take a terrible toll on the donor's assets.

Charities like lead trusts because they get income immediately and regularly for the life of the trust. The lead trust, like its unitrust siblings, can also be modified with certain customizations, such as annuitizing payments.

Trust Considerations and Drawbacks

So why wouldn't everyone fund a charitable remainder trust or a charitable lead trust? Why don't we see more of them? It's hard to prove a negative, i.e. why someone chooses not to do something, but there are some downsides to a charitable remainder unitrust that need to be considered.

- It is irrevocable. To qualify as a charitable remainder trust, the donor cannot change his or her mind. While there are ways to change or add charitable remainder interests, the bottom line is the donor has to be certain of intentions, because once started, it cannot be undone. In my experience this is the biggest reason why would-be donors choose not to fund one.

- It can be expensive. It costs money to write the trust and to run it. The trust will almost always have expenses and costs. Depending on the trust, who the trustee is, and the assets within it, these costs can be significant.

- To work, the remainder trust must be efficient. The expenses and costs of investing make remainder trusts generally unattractive at smaller funding amounts. Depending on the investment advisor the donor uses, the minimum starting amount could be $1 million or more. Most large banks that run trust departments won't administer one valued at less than this amount. Some smaller banks and nimble investment advisors might act as trustee or investment advisor/manager for a lesser amount, but the funding amount is still in the hundreds of thousands of dollars for most.

Even with these disadvantages, the charitable remainder trust and its variations should be a part of every planned giving program. There are simply too many situations that call for these wonderful giving vehicles and software providers have made illustrating them relatively easy.

It's regrettable that few donors take advantage of them. If more people knew of all that remainder trusts might offer, we would see more of them. Maybe one day.

If a donor is considering a remainder trust but does not like the expenses involved, ask them to consider a charitable gift annuity. It has many of the same benefits, but the donor does not administer it. It is common for someone to go very far towards starting a unitrust and end up funding a gift annuity instead.

In closing, remember how this chapter and trust history started. Trusts began with a property owner entrusting someone to manage it in the absence of the owner. It is a relationship. It is *always a relationship.*

All of these trust options, and even the taxation of the trust types, are all just ways of identifying and specifying the relationship between the donor, the life beneficiaries and the charitable beneficiary.

A good gift officer will listen to the donor; work with the donor's advisor(s), and offer trust solutions that fit a donor's particular needs and goals. You now have enough knowledge to know some basic options and to ask the right questions to your donors and to their advisors.

To Recap:

- Trusts can make gifts to charity without being a "charitable trust."

- Charitable Remainder Trusts and Charitable Lead Trusts are special trusts the government recognizes that offer donors incentives and opportunities to give to charity with income tax and capital gains tax benefits.

- Trusts are treated like people. They have a "lifespan," a tax ID number and must file annual returns with the government.

Chapter 6   Property Gifts

A List Full of Dollars

- If They Own it, They Will Want to Give it to You
- Art is in the Eye of the Beholder, but the IRS Judges its Worth
- You Don't Have to Take it All; and Likely Don't Want to

People will try to Give You Anything and Everything

The world of cars, planes, and diamond rings will probably not bring you the biggest gifts of your career. However, it is in this land of rings and things where all your best stories will come. Welcome to the world of personal property.

Personal property is anything you can own that is not an interest in real property. It can be tangible or intangible.

- Tangible is property you can touch.

- Intangible is property you cannot touch.

Real property, also known as real estate, is any interest in land. Real property is different than personal property and is important enough that it gets different treatment by the IRS and accordingly, deserves and receives its own chapter in this book.

In a perfect world, gifts of property, both real and personal, would probably not be a planned gift. But because of tradition or because no one else wants to handle them, they almost always arrive under the banner of planned giving.

That's fine because this is also an opportunity for the person taking the call to be a hero both to the donor and to the charity. I love helping donors with gifts of property and I suspect you do, or you soon will. Besides, gifts of property, real or personal, can be a source of significant giving.

The Wild World
of Property Gifts

Personal property gifts tend to be a mixed bag of opportunity and headache. Most charities prefer not to solicit or even accept gifts of anything other than cash, or maybe stock. But gifts of property can be useful; either because the nonprofit uses it (a gift of art to an art gallery) or can sell it and use the proceeds.

A lot of wealth can be tied up in personal property items, so it is worthwhile to be prepared to accept them. They can be worth a lot of money.

Speaking of money, that's one of the trickiest aspects of in-kind gifts. How much is the gift worth? With cash or even stock, it's fairly easy to determine value. But how much is that plane worth? What about that antique plow? If beauty is in the eye of the beholder then value is in the eye of the IRS and it does not always see things the way the donor does.

The important thing to remember about value is that with any charitable donation, the amount of the gift, and reporting it to the IRS for tax purposes, is always the responsibility of the donor. The charity does not set the value, *ever*. How much is that blouse worth? We don't know. How much is that pick-up truck worth? We don't know.

Some donors will expect us to tell them and even help them evaluate the worth of possible donations. While we can point them in the right direction, *it is always the donor's responsibility to value a gift.*

Gifts of property have another important side. Often the donor has an emotional attachment to "things" that the donor might not have for money or other liquid assets. Whenever a donor talks about giving some *thing*, handle it with extra care.

What Kind of Gifts Will People Want to Donate?

Among the items you might expect to receive, or be asked to receive in a career include:

- Cars

- Machinery

- Computers and other electronics

- Mobile homes or recreational vehicles

- Jewelry

- Artwork

- Airplanes

- Horses

Decisions, Decisions

People can and will give you, or attempt to give you almost anything imaginable. The questions are:

- Do you want to accept it?

- What is it worth?

- What can the nonprofit do with it?

- What are the tax ramifications for the donor?

Donations of cars and boats present special problems. Because of perceived abuses particular to donations of "junk" cars in recent years, there are special rules for donations of vehicles and for completing Form 8283.

Sometimes your donor's comic book collection is worth thousands of dollars. Sometimes you couldn't get $5 for it at the best garage sale. But the key to all property gifts of any size is to determine why the donor wants to give it to you and what you can do with it once you accept it.

Learning what to accept and not accept is a skill you are always improving. With the words in this chapter, my goal is to shorten that learning curve for you considerably. To help, here are a few terms you need to know, if you don't recognize them already.

- Real Property– Lawyer talk for "real estate." Land. Dirt. Could be downtown or down on the farm. Could be a small parcel on the beach or thousands of acres in the heartland. We'll explore real property in more depth in the next chapter. It could also be an interest, such as 50% ownership or maybe a leasehold.

- Personal Property– Something you own that is not land. Personal property is divided into two types, tangible and intangible. Personal property can be worthless or worth everything. It all depends, like all property, how much other people are willing to pay for it if they could buy it.

- Tangible Personal Property– Property you can touch. This would include diamond rings, computers, horses, artwork, a china set, baseball card collection, plane, car or boat.

- Intangible Personal Property– Property that could be described as something owned but not visible. It could be the right to receive royalties for writing a book or movie.

Could be the Colonel's recipe of *11 secret herbs and spices*, or the formula for Coca-Cola. Intangible personal property also includes things like business goodwill, partnerships, patents, and copyrights.

What Property Should You Accept?

The answer to this question is deceptively simple. Accept something that your organization can sell easily or use seamlessly for your mission. If you can't use it directly or can't sell it quickly, then you probably should not accept it. Knowing and understanding this rule is simple, but following is not always easy.

There's another catch, too; one that only experience and not economics can teach. If the donor has emotional strings around the gift that almost choke it, then you probably don't want the gift either. And donors are not always quick to let you know how attached they are to the property they are considering donating. Listen carefully to the donor for clues as to the donor's true feelings. Be especially carefully when the donor attempts to impose unrealistic or overly burdensome restrictions on the gift.

When a donor is giving something to your charity with conditions such as, "It can never be sold," or, "I expect you to use this for such and such a purpose," then think twice about accepting it. You are getting more than you bargained for – and candidly, most likely more than you want.

Be especially cautious when you hear comments such as:

- "I'll give you my artwork as long as you promise to display it at the entrance to campus forever."

- "You can have my house, but only the president of the organization can use it."

What it's Worth and what the Donor Thinks it's Worth can be Vastly Different

Here's an example of a common problem. A donor wants to give you a painting that he paid $2,000 for ten years ago. He was "promised" by the artist when he purchased it that it was really worth $10,000 and would only go up in value. The donor believes the painting is worth tens of thousands of dollars, because it was purchased on that premise. However, despite several efforts, the donor has been unable to sell it for even as little as $500.

The donor attributes the lack of a sale to poor marketing or more likely, uninformed buyers. So, the donor says you should have it instead. Of course, the donor fully intends to take an income tax deduction for the value of the painting, which in his mind is $25,000. The donor will be upset if you don't proudly display it or sell it for anything less than $30,000.

Speaking of art, this is an area the IRS is particularly fond of scrutinizing. Donations of art and an accompanying claimed large income tax deductions are one of the quickest ways to trigger an audit. For that reason alone, donors should take great care when claiming a tax deduction for donated art.

Valuing Gifts and Tax Forms Related to In-Kind Donations

Unfortunately, what a donor thinks a painting is worth and its true value can be as far apart as a Rembrandt masterpiece and a kindergartner's first attempt at finger painting. Valuing a donation for tax purposes can be tricky and sometimes a little complicated.

To help keep values clear, the IRS developed Form 8283 (and Form 8282) to control donations of in-kind property.

Form 8283

The IRS noticed a tendency to overvalue in-kind donations. Increasingly, it seemed donors were taking liberties when valuing donations for tax purposes. The government's primary solution was Form 8283.

When a donor gives something in-kind (something other than cash), the donor must value it if the donor wants to use the donation as an income tax deduction. A donor must file Form 8283 with the donor's tax return if the amount of the claimed deduction for all noncash gifts is more than $500. If it is more than $5,000 (except for some publicly traded securities) the donor must complete section B of the Form, along with a qualified appraiser.

Appraisers must have accreditation from a recognized professional appraisal organization or meet other minimal education requirements. The appraiser must also do this routinely for pay and has to be in good standing with the IRS. The IRS wants donors to know it takes in-kind donations seriously.

When the IRS finds a problem with the appraiser or appraisal it can and has reduced the value of the donation to zero without ever reaching discussion or valuation of the item's worth. Bottom line: if a donor talks about giving you art or some other personal property, make sure the donor understands whether it is for a related or unrelated use (more on this on page 112), and advise the donor to get an appraisal from someone who does this regularly, routinely and is in good standing with the IRS.

Form 8282

Form 8283 works with a companion form known as Form 8282, which is also known as the Tattletale Form. Unlike Form 8283 that is completed by the donor (or the donor and the donor's appraiser), Form 8282 is completed and filed by the charity.

When a charity disposes of a gift within three years of its donation, it must complete this form. The form is called the Tattletale Form, because the charity must disclose important information *including the sale price* if the charity sold the item. If the sale price reported by the charity varies significantly from what the donor claimed on the donor's tax return, you can be sure the IRS will be calling the donor to ask tough questions.

Anytime anyone donates anything other than cash or stock, make sure you point the donor to Form 8283 and encourage the donor to hire competent counsel and an appraiser if appropriate.

Why Starving Artists Starve

If a collector owns a painting genuinely worth $1 million and contributes it to charity, the collector has a $1 million deduction. If the artist who created the painting donates it to the charity, the artist has a deduction of $50 or so dollars – the cost of canvas and paint. Why? Legend says we have Richard Nixon to thank for that.

The story goes that Nixon donated his manuscripts to a library and took a tax deduction of $1 million. Congress was so upset it sought to end donations like this, or similar circumstances where donors would "paint a deduction" for themselves. So, Congress enacted special rules so that art in the hands of the artist that created it could only be valued at the basis when donating it to charity.

The basis is the amount the artist or creator paid for the paint, canvas or any other materials that went into making the art. Today the rule is artists take the deduction of the Fair Market Value of the art or the artist's basis, whichever is *lesser*.

Abuse in the Use of Deductions

Many of the rules we have now result from specific abuse, or perceived abuse in the past. For example, there is a special section on taxidermy. In the past some creative hunters took extravagant safaris and brought back stuffed animals (the real kind, not the ones you win at the carnival) for presentation to museums. They claimed the expense of the safari to be an income tax deduction. Today there are detailed, strict limits on gifts of taxidermy, in part, as a result from practices like this in the past.

What the IRS takes, the IRS also gives. The IRS website has easy-to-follow instructions and forms for valuing in-kind and personal property gifts. Search the IRS with the important terms then add the words "Form," or "Publication" to your query for more direct results. IRS Publication 526 is especially helpful for information about nonprofit donations.

Related Use

The IRS looks at donations of personal property through a special lens called "Related Use." The IRS says a donor is entitled to an income tax deduction for the fair market value of a donated item if the use of it is related to the stated tax-exempt mission of the organization.

If a donor gives a painting worth $1 million to an art museum that displays that kind of art, then the donor is entitled to value the art at $1 million for income tax deduction purposes. (Importantly that value is determined by a qualified appraiser and submitted properly with Form 8283 as detailed above.)

However, if a gift of artwork worth $1 million is given to a zoo that does not display artwork, then the IRS limits the donor's deduction to the *lesser* of the donor's costs basis or the fair market value. So even if the artwork is worth $1 million but the donor paid $50,000 for it, the donor can only take a $50,000 deduction. This is true even if the artwork is donated to the zoo for an upcoming gala to be auctioned – and it makes $2 million at auction.

The IRS is peculiarly particular about gifts of property and each type of property has special rules. I have tried to prepare you by using tips and examples of some of the most common donations you will encounter, but even so these laws change often, especially in niche areas when a particular case comes up or certain headlines demand and end to abuse.

If an organization accepts personal property and then sells, exchanges or otherwise disposes of it before the last day of the taxable year, the IRS treats it as an unrelated use, even if it is exactly in line with the organization's charitable purpose.

To overcome this presumption, the IRS imposes strict requirements on the charity to demonstrate why it was a related use. If your organization accepts personal property that is for a related use, plan on keeping it a while.

Intangible and Intellectual Property

Certain donors may also wish to make a gift of intellectual property rights. Simply put, intellectual property is anything created by someone's mind. The government recognizes ownership rights in music, books, plays, movies, patents or any number of things that can generate income from the creative spark of the mind. And if intellectual property can be worth something, then it is something that can be given to charity.

The IRS limits the value (for income tax deduction purposes) of intangible property to the *lesser* of the fair market value or the donor's basis in the property. The IRS applies this rule to copyrights, trademarks, trade names, trade secrets, know-how, software and other similar property.

Be sure to check and be careful in this area. The IRS has exceptions to the rule, especially in the areas of some software and copyright donations. It gets complicated when the donor intends to keep an income stream from the donated property.

Gifts of intellectual property are rare and the laws regarding them change often – especially when the IRS senses abuse in certain areas. So anytime anyone wants to give you something that you cannot touch (keeping in mind a book or sheet music is only a depiction of the real object and not the object itself) engage an expert immediately. But know that intellectual property gifts can exist and remain a possibility for that special donor with a special intent for the right charity.

To Recap:

- Almost anything anyone can own can be given to charity.

- No contribution of cash or any monetary donation is valid without a receipt.

- Any contribution valued at $250 or more requires a receipt from the charity at the time of donation.

- Any contribution valued at $500 or more (other than cash) must have a receipt meeting certain requirements, and the donor must complete and file Form 8283.

- Any contribution valued at $5,000 or more (other than cash or publicly traded securities) must be substantiated by the donor with a qualified appraisal by a qualified appraiser. The donor must also complete and file Form 8283.

- Gifts of personal property present special valuation issues, and gifts of intangible personal property present even greater valuation issues that must be handled carefully by the donor and by the charity.

Chapter 7   Real Estate

Lands of Opportunity

- Give Me Land, Lots of Land
- There is More to Land than Meets the Eye
- Tips for Looking at Land Donations

Land and the Bundle of Sticks

In law school one of the first concepts they teach is that ownership of land is best described as a bundle of sticks. When we wholly own land we have all the sticks related to that land. One stick is the right to live on the property. Another might be the right to extract oil or minerals.

There are many rights associated with land. However, none of us really ever own 100% of land. The government holds some of the sticks in the form of zoning laws, taxation and easements that prevent us from full enjoyment of our property. While we never own all the sticks, that doesn't mean we can't own plenty of them.

Giving away, or not having some of the sticks in the bundle is not necessarily a bad thing. I cannot put my hot tub, for example, at the corner of my property because that's where a telephone pole and fire hydrant are. The rights to the land in that portion of my property partially belong to the utility company and water provider.

They have an easement in my property which means at some point I, or the person who owned the property before, gave up those sticks (rights) to them. Giving up a small corner of the property for electricity and fire prevention is a pretty good thing, so giving up those sticks, or rights, is typically something we gladly give away.

My homeowner's association may also have something to say about a hot tub in the corner of my property. Membership in and subjecting property to a homeowners association is another stick given from the bundle of property rights.

A Gift of Land is Not an
All or Nothing Proposition

Not to belabor the metaphor of sticks representing rights, it is important to know that ownership of land is not as simple as owning or not owning it. There are lots of rights and responsibilities that go with land, and an owner can choose to give some of those up – either for personal reasons or for a charitable donation.

If we live in a subdivision, we might give up certain sticks to the homeowners association. For example we can no longer paint our house bright pink without permission from the homeowners association, but then again, neither can our neighbor!

As we sell, assign or give away our rights to real property think about them as individual sticks in the big bundle of rights that come with owning property. With that in mind, people can give all or some of their rights in property to a charity. And the neat thing about the bundle of sticks metaphor is that it works with any type of property a donor may wish to give. And gifts of land can take many forms:

- A gift of a home (the most common)

- Undeveloped land

- Forest property (timberland)

- Commercial property

- Farm land

Each type of property presents special benefits and responsibilities for the owner. Each of those benefits and responsibilities also become those of the charity the moment it takes ownership.

Many organizations shy away from accepting gifts of real property or interests in it. That could be a mistake. At the same time, quickly accepting real property could be an even greater burden. While volumes could be written (and have been) on how to accept real property, there are some quick guidelines you can follow to keep you on track.

Attorneys are a Must with Property Transactions

Never accept any interest in real property without first talking with your attorney. Fortunately, there are many rituals and procedures associated with real property transactions so any reasonable donors attempting to give you property will understand when you say, "We need to run this by the attorney."

Tax Deductions for Gifts of Real Property

Donors can give you just about any interest in property. They can give you "full" ownership, which is known as fee simple. Donors might also split an interest; for example giving you the southern 20 acres of the 40 acre farm; or split another way, such as 50% ownership of the farm with the interest undivided, meaning you would not receive 20 specific acres, but rather half-ownership in all of them.

Of importance to the donor will be the income tax ramifications of giving the interest in real property. As you might expect, the larger the interest given, the larger the deduction will be. However, there are exceptions to the rule and some donations don't count at all.

When a "Gift" of Property
Produces no Deduction

One of the most surprising things to donors and charities is that the use of property does not qualify for a deduction at all. If a donor gives you the use of office space in a class A building that the donor could have otherwise rented out for thousands of dollars, the deduction is still zero. The donor is a nice person, but the IRS just doesn't recognize a deduction for the value of the free use of real property.

For those contributions that do result in a charitable income tax deduction, it is important for the donor to transfer ownership to the charity directly, and not sell the property with the intent on giving the proceeds to charity.

Although if the charity refuses ownership and it works for the donor, the donor may sell the property and give the charity cash and take an income tax deduction for the cash contribution. This works fine in some circumstances, especially when the property has depreciated or not appreciated much; or if there are good reasons for the charity not to own it.

Property must be Owned Longer than
One Year to be Long Term Capital Gain

If a donor gives property the donor has owned less than one year, the IRS considers it "ordinary income" property and the donor's deduction is limited to what the donor paid for it plus any costs the donor has paid for the property during ownership. This rule is true for all appreciated property, even personal property.

Assuming though, that the donor has held the property longer than a year, real property can be a great asset to give, and a great asset for a charity to receive. As such the donor avoids capital

119

gains tax that would otherwise be due if the donor sold the property.

Determining the Value of the Property

It is up to a qualified appraiser to tell the donor what that interest in donated property is worth. For example, if a donor owns one-third of an undivided interest in the property and gives it to charity, the appraisal will take into account that the ownership interest is a minority one and the charity is becoming a "partner" in ownership of the land with only one vote out of three in the ownership of it.

Mortgage Messiness

Mortgages can be a real problem. If a donor wants to give you property with a mortgage on it, special care is needed. The deduction will be reduced by the amount of the outstanding debt on the mortgage. The IRS considers the donor to have received a benefit from the relief of that mortgage obligation and the donor has experienced a gain.

If the property has an appraised fair market value of $100,000 and the donor has a $30,000 balance on the mortgage, the value of the donation is $70,000. This assumes the charity pays off the mortgage when accepting the property.

It does not end there. The donor may also have to pay capital gains or income taxes as a result of the donor's mortgage obligations being paid by the charity. All property transactions are complex, and ones with mortgages are especially difficult. Just know that if a mortgage is involved, it makes the likelihood of accepting the property much less certain, and the need for counsel absolutely certain!

The Bargain Sale

When a charity pays off a mortgage for a donor, it is really a form of a bargain sale. A more common bargain sale is when the donor sells the charity something at a price less than Fair Market Value.

A typical bargain sale would go something like this. The donor owns property worth $100,000 and wants to get rid of it while also doing something to benefit your charity. The donor cannot afford to give you the property outright, so the donor offers to sell it to your charity for $30,000.

Assuming you want this property and there are no reasons not to take it (such as environmental or other concerns) this could be great for both parties. The donor gets rid of the burden of owning the property, walks away with $30,000 cash and the charity, presumably, can sell the property for $100,000 making a "profit" of $70,000. Not bad.

In the example above, the donor receives an income tax deduction of $70,000. That represents the value of the property given outright to the charity. The $30,000 in the pocket of the donor will be subject to taxation in the same way as if the property had been sold at a fair market price, but only prorated to represent the bargain sale.

In this case the donor would pay capital gains on the difference between the fair market value and the basis prorated to only the $30,000 portion. Since 30,000 is 30% in this case, the donor would pay capital gains only on 30% of the difference between the donor's basis and the fair market value.

Donors Rarely Give
Real Property as their First Gift

The question: "Why does the donor want to give us this property," can be incredibly revealing. When talking about property, always ask the donor, "Why?" I have found the only property worth accepting is property owned by someone who has given other gifts before. This property is just another facet of an already healthy relationship.

Be wary of the newfound friend with real property to give you. Newfound friends are those who really don't have a connection with your nonprofit, but now want to give you their valuable, very valuable, incredibly valuable property because they just want to do some good with it.

If someone has never given to you before and suddenly wants to give you property, especially real property, be cautious. Why? People rarely make a genuine real property gift as their first gift. In as nice a way as possible, ask the donor about the property, and why the donor wants to give it to you. In many cases the donor will say something about trying to sell it for so-and-so number of years, but they just couldn't because [insert here one of a hundred rationalizations why the property did not sell]. After careful consideration, "they want to do something good with it," and want to give it your cause instead.

In most cases there is a very good reason why the property didn't sell. There is something wrong with it. Could be overpriced. Could be a dump. Could be simply worthless. Sadly, the real reason why the donor is giving it to you is because he or she is tired of dealing with it and would prefer to take an income tax deduction for it instead. The donor also wants to alleviate the bad feelings of not having a sale by feeling a little better by giving it to you.

If the donor had trouble selling it, so will your organization. The donor simply wants to transfer ownership, and the problems and headaches that go with it, to you. Don't fall for it. The donor may mean well and wish to salvage a bad situation, but unfortunately, giving it to charity rarely makes the donor feel better; especially when you start talking about a realistic valuation and tax deduction for the donor.

If you do accept it, the donor will likely want to take a very large deduction for it. The donor will be very upset to learn that it appraises for much less than the donor thinks it will.

Remember that if the donor had nothing emotionally invested in your organization before the donation, he or she will have no problems telling everyone and posting to every social media website; how unappreciative your organization is, and how it apparently squanders assets by not valuing them for "what they are worth." Not only did you receive a dog with fleas, but the dog bites you when you try to give it a bath!

Timeshares – a Special Warning

If a red alert flashed for any property it would be for timeshares. And you *will* get calls from people wanting to give you their timeshare units. Timeshare developers have very sophisticated selling techniques that make buyers believe *interval ownership* is the best "investment" anyone can make. They often tell buyers their units will always increase in value even though the developer plans to build an additional 1,000 units across the parking lot next year (that's 50,000 time share units in one building!).

The timeshare that was never a good investment for the donor will always be a problem for you. While some timeshares may have terrific value and great appreciation, this is one donation I have never found to be worth it– unless you want a unit as reward for your staff member or volunteer of the year, and your organization is prepared to pay and accept all the responsibilities that come with ownership.

When you do Choose to Accept Property

Assuming you have contacted counsel and you feel reasonably certain that accepting the property is best for you and for the donor, then do it. Property can be a wonderful gift. Follow counsel's advice, and be sure to purchase title insurance and protect yourself and your organization at every step.

Know What Lurks Beneath the Ground

Beside all the emotional and practical problems present with gifts of property, be especially carefully with environmental issues. Environmental problems can show up in areas where you least expect them. No property is immune from environmental concerns.

That simple house in the subdivision could be sitting on what was once a farm. Maybe a couple decades ago the farmer used to store or dump his extra pesticides in a hole that is now covered and in the middle of the donor's backyard. Maybe he gassed up the tractor from a diesel tank buried under what is now the donor's front yard.

Now that pit or that tank is starting to corrode enough where really nasty stuff is leaking into the groundwater. The farmer and his money are long gone. The donor has a sad and an unfortunate situation, but your organization cannot afford for it to become its problem.

If your organization owns the property, it owns the problem of cleaning this mess up. Worse yet, your liability for cleaning it up could continue forever, even after you sell it.

And while twenty years from now four or five different people or organizations may have owned the property, the one who discovers the problem will look to you to pay to clean it, because your organization likely has "deeper pockets" than any other person or entity that has owned the property since. So avoid environmental liabilities by looking at all property carefully before accepting ownership.

Some environmental issues that can cause trouble or cost lots of money to fix, include but are not limited to:

- Underground storage tanks (typically associated with farms, factories and gas stations).

- Unmarked graves or private cemeteries.

- Chemicals in the ground from factory, dry-cleaning or lumber operations.

- And unfortunately, today a growing problem with illicit drug production in homes resulting in severe chemical contamination.

Environmental problems can be expensive and extensive to clean up, and as such the government imposes tremendous liability to owners. Under federal law property owners can be responsible for paying the costs of cleaning the property even if the owner was not responsible for the pollution.

Anyone who owns the property at any time since the pollution might possibly be made to pay for it. So even if the charity owns the property for a day and sells it the next, years later the charity can be called upon to pay for cleaning it when contamination is found, and cleaning toxins out of property can be expensive. It has put well-funded private corporations out of business forever.

If your charity is seriously considering accepting a gift of real property or participating in a bargain sale to take ownership, your organization should take careful steps to investigate the environmental hazards that could be on the property.

The moment it appears a donor is serious about giving real property that you might want, alert your counsel to the potential property donation.

Although the attorney will lead the investigation here are some terms you might hear, and some you may want to use when recommending to your superiors to justify the need to hire counsel.

- A Phase I Environmental Survey of the property is a visual inspection of the land. Qualified inspectors will walk the land to look for clues as to past pollution or other concerns, as well as review the chain of ownership of the property for any possible red flags.

- A Phase II Environmental Survey involves testing soil samples and investigating behind walls and below the surface in more depth. A phase II might uncover hidden dangers such as creosol in the soil or asbestos in the walls.

- A Phase III Environmental Survey digs deeper, further and longer with more extensive sampling and testing.

Make sure you hire the right experts and let them advise whether a Phase I environmental inspection is sufficient or more research is warranted.

To-Do List

Here is a checklist for things to consider and discuss with your attorney and your leadership before accepting property:

- Does the charity want to keep the property or sell it? If the charity wants to sell it, is there a market for it?

- Exactly what interest in the property is the donor trying to give us?

- What interest does the donor own? (a title check will reveal this)

- Does the donor have title insurance?

- Are the taxes paid?

- Are there any interests out there (other sticks in the bundle) that might prevent us from doing what we want with the property?

- Is the property part of a lawsuit or other dispute?

- Is there a mortgage, lien or other encumbrance on the property?

- What will it cost for the charity to own the property (insurance upkeep, fees, etc.) and is this something it wants to do?

- Why does the donor want to give us this property?

- What is the environmental status of the property?

If you hear any of these words associated with real property you are considering accepting be extra careful: gas station, auto shop, dry cleaner, farm, or factory.

Ways of Giving and Receiving Real Property

The most common gift of property is an outright gift. Someone by deed or by will simply gives property to your charity. This happens all the time, and assuming there are no environmental concerns or liens on the property, this is a good gift.

Real property can be used in other ways, too.

Retained Life Estate

This is a common way of giving real property where the donor gives the "remainder" interest in the property to charity but retains the right to live there for life.

The donor (it can be husband and wife or whoever owns the property) agrees to give the property to the charity, and agrees to maintain it for life. The donor must cover all the routine costs such as lawn care, insurance and anything else one might expect in the normal upkeep and care of the property. The property passes automatically to the charity when the owner(s) die.

Even though the donor still lives in the property, that remainder interest has value and the donor is entitled to an income tax deduction the year that the donor gives that property interest to the charity.

It is up to the donor to work out that value with the donor's counsel and appraiser. The charity must decide it wants that remainder interest and is willing to approach the donor when and if necessary to make sure the property is maintained properly.

Interestingly, the donor does not have to live on the property. The donor's interest in the property is measured by the donor's life or donors' lives. This can work for any type of property. The donor can choose later to terminate his or her (or their) rights and give all rights to the charity early.

Real Property for a Gift Annuity

Let's say a donor wants to give you property in exchange for a gift annuity. If your organization permits it, why not? If you and the donor can come to agreement on the value of the property it's a fine way of funding a gift annuity.

I recommend the donor obtain three independent appraisals at the donor's expense and value the property as the average of the three. Then it is up to you and the donor to agree on a value for the gift annuity. Some organizations value the gift annuity at 80% of that agreed value.

An agreed value of 80% is a good choice because there will be expenses for the charity to own the land and maintain it. There will be costs to the charity to sell it, and there might be some time before the property is sold. The 20% provides a cushion to cover these expenses and helps make this a fair transaction for the donor and for the charity.

Real Property in a Trust

Placing property in a trust is a brilliant solution, assuming it is valuable enough to justify the cost of trust administration. Because the trust owns it and not the charity, the environmental concerns are usually lessened on the charity. The donor can choose a type of trust that works best for this land.

A unitrust with a flip provision can be used for property that may not be sold quickly or may not produce income for a few years (such as timber acreage where trees won't be harvested for a few years). Other trusts, too, offer different advantages. And as with other appreciated assets, when property is transferred to a trust the donor does not pay capital gains that would otherwise be due if the property were sold.

A Final Thought on Property

When a donor gives property to a charity, the donor will reap several rewards. First the donor has been paying taxes, insurance and other out-of-pocket expenses for owning it, perhaps for years. Those end with the donation.

Even better, by transferring it to a trust or gift annuity, the donor receives income tax and capital gains benefits as well as receiving a payment stream from an asset that might have been costing the donor money. Real property can be an effective and rewarding way for a donor to give substantially to charity.

To Recap:

- Real property can be a significant source of gifts for charity.

- People can give all kinds of property and interests in it to charity.

- Charities should always consult legal counsel when it appears a donor is serious about giving property.

- Mortgages, liens, taxes and environmental concerns all present traps for the donor and especially for the charity.

- Real property can be most effective when conveyed as part of a bargain sale or transferred to a trust or transferred in exchange for a gift annuity.

Chapter 8 Life Insurance & Retirement Plans

Easy but Forgotten Friends

- Life Insurance – The Most Underused Planned Gift
- Retirement Plans Make Easy and Efficient Planned Gifts
- IRA Rollovers – A New Way to Give

Life Insurance – an Easy, Yet Significant Planned Gift

There was a time in England when life insurance was more like a sport or outright gambling. You could choose a total stranger and buy a life insurance policy on his life. If he died, the insurance company owed you money.

Not unlike a modern casino bet, one could take out a policy on a famous person, betting he would not live for a certain number of years, months or even days.

As Parliament found this increasingly distasteful, it enacted laws in 1774 saying before one could take out a life insurance policy on another person's life, there had to be an "insurable interest."

That term and that concept remain with us. Today, states have special rules to allow charities to be the beneficiaries of life insurance policies, finding them to have an "insurable interest" in the lives of donors.

Life insurance is one of the most underused, but highly rewarding areas for nonprofits. When used properly, life insurance offers a tremendous boost to your bottom line.

Life insurance allows donors to make large or extra-large gifts for relatively little money. One large insurance policy can cover the entire annual budget of a small or medium-sized nonprofit.

Life insurance companies are highly competitive and life insurance has rarely been as great a bargain as it is today. Moreover, life insurance policies have multiple benefits for the donor.

If the donor gives a policy that has been held for a few years, the donor can receive an income tax deduction for the present value of the policy. And the donor can make what are essentially premium payments to the charity and get tax deductions for them, too.

The key for any life insurance gift to be effective is for the donor to make the charity the owner and beneficiary of the policy. This means the charity now has the relationship with the insurance company and makes all decisions on the policy (although the death benefit is still based on the life and death of the donor).

Life Insurance Premiums and Income Tax Deductions

When the charity is owner of a life insurance policy, it is responsible for making the premium payments, if there are any left to be made on the policy. As the charity makes payments, the common practice is for the charity to pay the premium then ask the donor to make a gift to the charity for the same amount as the premium.

Even though the charity is asking the donor for a donation that is equal to the premium that is due, the donor is not paying the premium. The donor is simply making a gift that happens to be in the same amount as the premium the charity just paid.

As donors give to the charity in an amount equal to the premium, it counts as a cash gift to the charity. It really is simple. If a charity pays a premium of $1,000 and asks the donor for $1,000 and the donor gives it, the donor has made a gift of $1,000.

This gives the donor an opportunity to not only make a big difference with the death benefit, but also pick up some annual tax deductions along the way. Incidentally, because the death benefit never was and never is part of the donor's estate, it is also not eligible for any income or estate tax deductions.

Pitching Life Insurance, Catching the Business

There is one thing you need to know about life insurance that is different from every other gift; even from every other planned gift. Life insurance is the only gift that needs a salesperson to make it happen.

Every other gift can be made without any sales assistance. Life insurance is a product and products cannot be sold without a sale, so let's talk first about the product and then about the people who sell them.

There are thousands of insurance companies in the United States that can sell a life insurance policy. Each has dozens or hundreds of agents, all wanting to sell them. Most, if not all of them, derive at least part of their living by commission.

If they sell no policies they make no money. However, if they sell a lot of policies, they can make a substantial income. For that reason there is a great deal of motivation for people to sell you, your organization, and your donors on the idea of life insurance.

All life insurance is a promise by a company that when a particular person dies, the company will send a check to the person (or people) the insured person designated. How do insurance companies make their product more attractive than the insurance company down the street? Unlike colas or fried chicken, there is no secret recipe, no special sauce; just money paid when someone dies.

From time to time, I get a call from an agent telling me of an innovation in life insurance. Some even involve investors "lined up" to help the donor pay the premium. Run away from calls like this. You do not have enough time to sort out these calls. I have never taken a call like that worth taking!

I recall one week when three different offices from one large financial firm called me trying to sell me the exact same life insurance scheme. Each tried to convince me that although they were several states away they could handle all my donor's life insurance needs. If it sounds too good to be true, it probably is.

Insurance companies and their agents are always thinking of new ways to make themselves look better than the others. Some of the innovations do make some policies more attractive to some people under certain conditions. However, *do not* be distracted by the sales pitch. Picking the right underwriter, agent and policy is beyond the scope of this book, assuming one could relate such words on paper to anyone who might read them.

Life Insurance Works

Even with the clutter created by mass marketing, life insurance remains an effective gift vehicle. With life insurance there are only three things you need to consider, or to advise your donor to consider for a charitable gift:

- What is the fiscal reputation of the underwriter?

- How much money is the death benefit for this policy?

- What would the premiums be? Life insurance is a competitive field, so encourage your donor to shop around.

Types of Life Insurance

Insurance companies essentially offer two types of life insurance: term and whole life. Because there are hundreds of insurance companies, they all compete to offer some advantage over the others. As a result there are dozens of variations of each type of policy, but they all fall into one of these two basic categories.

- A term policy is a policy that exists for a *term* of years. Generally less expensive than whole life, term insurance is designed to protect families upon the accidental death of the family breadwinner(s) during prime earning years.

- Whole life insurance is probably what most people think of when they hear "life insurance." Whole life is a sum paid to a beneficiary after the death of the insured person. For planned giving purposes, charities are more concerned about whole life.

A life insurance policy is only as good as its underwriter. Only use underwriters with a good reputation for customer service and with a stellar credit rating.

Some Handy Life Insurance Definitions

Agent: A person or corporation acting on behalf of an insurance company to solicit, sell or aid in the formation of life insurance policies or any business related to it (such as collecting premiums or responding to insureds' questions).

Cash Surrender Value: If a life insurance policy owner chooses to "cash in" a policy prior to the insured's death, this is the amount the insurance company will pay. The value changes and generally grows larger the longer the policy is held and as premiums are paid.

Death Benefit: The face amount of the life insurance policy to be paid to the designated beneficiaries upon the death of the insured.

Policy: The written contract between the underwriter (the insurer) and the insured, detailing the rights and responsibilities of each.

Second to Die Policy: Life Insurance, which pays the death benefit only after both lives insured under the policy have died. Second to Die policies can offer significant premium savings, even for older donors.

Term Life Insurance: Issued by an insurance company for a term of years. Typical terms are 10, 15, 20, 25, or 30 years.

Underwriter: a generic term for the insurance company that writes an insurance policy.

Whole Life: Insurance for the "whole life" of the insured with the benefit of the policy paid upon the insured's death.

We have only scratched the surface of life insurance with this discussion. Life insurance offers relatively large gift possibilities with comparatively little money from the donor.

Retirement Plans: the Easiest Planned Gifts of All

One of the easiest ways to raise money for your organization is to remind people to include it as a beneficiary of their retirement plan. Donors can name your organization as a beneficiary of their IRA, 401(k) or 403(b). All they have to do is call their plan administrator and ask for a change of beneficiary form. Then when the donor dies, any funds left in the retirement plan go to your organization.

When asking the donor to make your organization a beneficiary of a retirement plan or other financial account, let them know the space on the form for writing the charity's name will likely be very small. Almost all forms are designed for people's names and not the (usually) longer names of nonprofits. Don't let this be a surprise or discouragement to your donor.

Perhaps the greatest benefit of a gift from an IRA, 401(k) or 403(b) is its utter simplicity. There is no need for an attorney or accountant. Although, of course, the donor should ensure any action complies with the donor's professional advisors' advice!

To make the change and leave hundreds of thousands of dollars to your organization, it is as simple as writing your organization's name on the form or on a computer screen. The donor can also split the gift between beneficiaries. All the donor must do is follow the procedures established by the plan administrator. Let your donor know that the retirement plan assets can be split between family members, friends and charities in any way the donor wishes.

Rollover to a Better Gift

Keeping in mind that the goal is for your charity to be the beneficiary of an IRA or other retirement plan, there is another more immediate way of using these for a charitable gift. It is called the "IRA rollover," or "charitable rollover," and it is getting a lot of attention, deservedly so.

> *Ever wonder why we call retirement plans "401(k)," or "403(b)"? It is because these numbers refer to the sections of the United States Code that created them.*

An IRA, or Individual Retirement Account, is a financial account in which an individual can invest pre-tax earnings so it can grow tax-free until retirement. The individual does not pay income tax on the funds until the individual withdraws them.

There are two important ages with IRAs: 59½ and 70½. If you withdraw money from your IRA before age 59½ not only will you pay income tax on that withdrawal, but you will also pay a penalty. The government designed the IRA to encourage saving for retirement and penalizes the individual for premature withdrawals.

From the government's point of view, those funds have grown for years or decades without being taxed. The government wants the income taxes associated with those funds. The trade-off for the ability to grow the funds all those years tax-free is that the government *requires* you to start withdrawing them at age 70½.

When the donor reaches that age, the government has a formula based on the donor's age that requires a certain amount of money from the individual's IRA to be withdrawn. This is called the Required Minimum Distribution.

The individual still gets the money, but as the money is withdrawn (distributed), the IRS is paid income tax on the withdrawal. For our purposes, know that a donor can withdraw funds from an IRA at age 59½ and *must* take a distribution at age 70½ and older. It is the Required Minimum Distribution (or RMD) that has been the subject of hot debate and an off-and-on source for charitable donations.

In 2006, Congress passed the Pension Protection Act. The Act allowed donors to do something they could never do before: give money from their IRA directly to charity. There were some rules.

- The donor had to contact the plan administrator and ask the administrator to make the distribution directly to the charity. The money never touches the donor's hands.

- The donor had to be 59½.

- The charitable contribution was limited to $100,000 per individual (a husband and wife could each donate $100,000 from their IRAs if they each had an IRA).

- The contribution could not be used to fund a split interest gift such as a charitable gift annuity.

- The distribution to charity counted against the donor's Required Minimum Distribution.

- The donor does not receive an income tax deduction.

The IRA rollover was a welcome benefit for older donors with IRAs who would rather not take a distribution from their IRAs. Perhaps they had enough other money or just didn't need a distribution, and did not want to take it and owe the accompanying tax bill. This was an excellent way of satisfying the Required Minimum Distribution, while benefitting a favored charitable cause.

In the years since the Act passed, the IRA rollover has come into and out of favor with Congress, available some years, unavailable others. Check to see if the IRA rollover is valid for you and your donors. I hesitate to even mention whether it is in existence as of this writing because Congress tends to pass this at the last moment, or even as it did on December 31, 2012, retroactively. Always check.

IRA Rollovers are for IRAs Only

As of the date of publication, IRAs are the only retirement vehicle that is or ever has been available for a donor to make a tax-free transfer to a qualified charity.

While a 403(b) and a 401(k) are not eligible, if that is what the donor has, ask the donor to see about transferring funds to an

IRA, thus making them eligible for an IRA rollover–if it exists that year.

Even if the donor does not already have an IRA, it is okay to open one for the sole purpose of transferring funds to it for a charitable IRA rollover. Check with counsel before talking with donors.

Closing Thoughts

Life insurance and retirement plans are an easy and excellent source of giving. Donors can fund life insurance with relatively little money that results in significant gifts for charity.

Gifts from retirement accounts are even easier. All a donor has to do is call their plan administrator and ask to name your organization as a beneficiary.

Whether with life insurance or a retirement plan, the donor should check with the donor's advisor (not the life insurance agent who has a vested interest in the policy) to ensure the gift is in line with the donor's plan. Making a gift with life insurance or retirement plan involves relatively little paperwork and none of the legal formalities of wills or trusts and the administrative costs associated with them.

To Recap:

- Donors should name your organization the owner and beneficiary of their life insurance policy to get full tax benefits.

- When the charity makes life insurance premium payments, the donor can send a gift to the charity in the same amount and receive an income tax deduction.

- Gifts from retirement accounts are as easy as changing one line in a form supplied by the donor's retirement plan administrator.

- The IRA rollover, when available, allows a donor to make a distribution directly from the donor's IRA to charity and satisfies the donor's Required Minimum Distribution, within certain guidelines.

Chapter 9   Putting it All Together

See the World from the Donor's Point of View

- It's Always about Relationships
- Follow-up and Follow-through
- It's Always the Donor's Money

Why The Wizard of Oz is the
Best Planned Giving Movie Ever Made

Of all the movies about planned giving, perhaps the best-planned giving movie ever made was *The Wizard of Oz*. I bet you never thought of the classic movie in terms of planned giving.

Maybe it was not the intention of L. Frank Baum when he wrote the book in 1900 or Victor Fleming's focus when he made it into a motion picture. But of all the many movies about planned giving, it just might be the best planned giving movie ever made.

The movie begins with the *death* of a witch and a controversy over who will *inherit* the ruby slippers (they were silver slippers in the book, but the ruby color showed up better on film). The story unfolds as a young girl and her needy friends pursue a donor, the Wizard, who is the only one who can fill each of their needs.

The rewards come only after the girl and her friends prove to the donor that their mission is a worthy one. He may not be the donor they expect him to be, but ultimately their in-kind gift of a witch's broom results in fulfillment of their mission.

Okay, maybe it's a stretch to call *The Wizard of Oz* a planned giving movie. Or maybe it isn't. There is another valuable lesson in the movie. It has to do with the value of following your heart; listening to your instincts and realizing you know more than you think you do. Did you ever notice that well-meaning friends and advisors and "common knowledge" can often be wrong – even dangerous?

"... Some people without brains do an awful lot of talking... don't they?" – Scarecrow; "Yes, I guess you're right." – Dorothy.

In *The Wizard of Oz*, Dorothy and her friends are told the path that will take them home is paved with gold bricks. However, in the end they (and we) learn everything Dorothy and her companions needed was not in front of them. It was *inside* them the whole time.

What everyone misses in the movie version of the story is that many well-wishing friends, and even foes, are happy to give advice. They send the heroes on a long and winding journey fraught with peril that was totally unnecessary. That path was the obvious one, the one more traveled, and the easiest choice because it was all anyone knew. So, off they went.

Why does everyone follow the yellow brick road? It's easy. It's there. It has its own catchy tune. Yet, the characters have to go through a long and arduous journey (the book is much darker and scarier than the movie) to make it home.

Sometimes life provides stories more colorful than the movies.

During filming of *The Wizard of Oz* moviemakers were looking for a costume for actor Frank Morgan to wear in his role as Professor Marvel. The script called for a jacket that had the look of "grandeur gone to seed." They found such a jacket in a second-hand store (*another* charitable connection).

What they did not know, until Morgan later turned the pocket inside out, was that the jacket had the name "L. Frank Baum" embroidered in its lining. The velvet-collared jacket worn in the movie by Frank Morgan had been donated to the thrift shop by Baum's widow after her husband's death.

Others will not always Give you Good Advice

Take note of the yellow brick road, but to find your way home, don't listen only to the crowd. To find the greatest gifts don't take the road everyone else has already walked. Follow your instincts, follow your donors, and listen to your heart.

Follow your Heart and Not the Crowd

The crowd will tell you another ball, another gala, another auction is the way to prosperity. After all, that's what *they have done* for years. But the truth is, while these transaction-based techniques can bring in some money, they don't bring in nearly enough. They provide no lasting funding. They are here and then they are gone.

"Every client you keep is one less
that you need to find." – Nigel Sanders

Planned giving provides sustaining, charity-building funds. When you set your mind on where sustainable funding is, everything else falls into place. With a good planned giving program, or even a good planned giving effort, your events, annual fund, and all facets of fundraising will succeed.

When people make a planned gift, they also increase their annual and major gifts. They do so because with their planned gift(s) they have invested in your cause.

When "experts" tell you donors don't want to hear a planned giving message, ask the source of their data. Often the person making the statement does not know what a planned gift is, what it does, or could do.

They typically are speaking for themselves under the pretense of knowing what's best for others. Be careful and diplomatic when dealing with such people, but know your donors are smarter than that.

They want to hear a planned giving message for many reasons, foremost of which is the indication that the charity is mature enough to have staying power and the foresight to plan for the future.

Think of it like this. The nonprofit that depends on events (walks, runs, zombie dances, bake sales, etc.) is always looking for the next walker, runner, zombie, and cake-eater. It takes a lot of energy to raise not a lot of money. You are always looking for the next golfer, sponsor and team to replace the one that golfed, sponsored and walked the last event. It is a cruel, thankless and unending cycle.

If you have a roster of people who love you and believe in you, you don't have to find replacements. The ones in front of you, the ones who gave yesterday, will give tomorrow.

With planned giving, your effort and energy is spent on maintaining relationships rather than trying to always build new ones. Doesn't that sound healthier and easier? And by the way, compare the average donation from a walk participant to that of a planned giver. Depending on which statistics you use, the scale is approximately ten-to-one or as high as a thousand to one. The average planned gift is measured in tens of thousands of dollars. The average event gift is measured in tens of dollars.

Relationships

While the bulk of this book has been dedicated to the technical aspects of planned giving, it is the relationships and the forming and nurturing of them that is where it all comes together. We must give before we might get.

While planned giving vehicles are important and we need to know them, it is the *relationship* between nonprofit and donor that is at the heart of planned giving. In more practical terms, it is the relationship between the donor and gift officer that matters.

Let's spend a few moments examining how we can take what we have learned and look at the best ways we can take these skills and ideas into the living rooms and offices of our donors in the best ways possible and in a light most favorable for our donors.

To Protect and Serve

Successful planned giving officers have one thing in common. They are genuinely nice people. They are the kind of person anyone would want to spend a couple of hours with in a living room.

Be the person that others want to spend time with.

Be nice.

It may sound silly, but charitable giving is never, *ever* an economic decision. It is an emotional one. There is a maxim I heard years ago that I share with you. People make decisions emotionally and justify them intellectually.

This is true of multi-millionaires. This is true of little old ladies who saved up pennies in a mayonnaise jar to give to your cause. There are people who might disagree with this statement, but many more who live by it.

If it were not true, everyone would drive only the most basic car, live in the most modest homes, and wear only functional clothing. People live emotionally. People buy emotionally. People give emotionally.

> An ounce of loyalty is worth a pound of cleverness. – Elbert Hubbard

Passion Drives Every Donation

Consider this. Even though there are many great and powerful planned giving techniques, none offer the donor a way of giving away money and ending up with more than when the donor started. Even the most sophisticated charitable giving plan ends with the donor giving away more than the donor keeps!

It is a fruitless exercise to convince donors they are financially better off by giving money to your cause. They just aren't. But that's okay. By giving to you they are emotionally better off, and you cannot put a price on happiness.

The one thing we can do is make sure the donor gives in a way that is satisfying economically and invigorating emotionally. And with proper giving techniques we can provide income and life insurance for the donor and donor's family and provide for all the donor's charitable intentions.

I offer you what I call Olson's Law on Giving:

A donor will only give when the emotional satisfaction of giving an asset outweighs the comfort of keeping it.

Except that's what I used to call Olson's Law on Giving, then I changed one word, and it made all the difference.

A donor will always give when the emotional satisfaction of giving an asset outweighs the comfort of keeping it.

There is some threshold every donor has that governs whether a gift will be made or not. It is different for every person and it probably differs a little day-to-day for the same person. However, if the donor crosses it, a gift is made. If not: no gift.

Why we give and what we give is a deeply personal decision. As gift officers the best we can do is listen and respond to donors with portions of our mission that stimulate that donor's charitable senses and satisfy any economic concerns or goals they have. Donors give for their reasons, not ours, and certainly not for our needs.

The only rule you need to know about fundraising is one that has been around a long time. Treat donors the way you would want to be treated!

Getting Started

One of the greatest benefits of purposeful improvement of a planned giving program is that it is so easy to start or grow what you already have. Even if you have never completed a planned gift before, your planned giving donors are probably already right in front of you already.

So how do we identify them? Where are they? Where do we begin?

- First, get the message out to all your donors, especially those 60 and over that your organization can be supported through a gift in a will, trust, or other planned gift.

- If there are board members, key donors, or staff members that are life insurance agents, attorneys, accountants, or financial advisors, seek their input and advice on how to increase planned gifts to the organization.

- Make sure all your donors are receiving all mailings from your organization. Sometimes we send only solicitation-oriented materials to certain donors. Make sure they also receive mission-related updates. Solicitation materials get thrown away. Mission updates generate donations.

- Spend a little time each day looking at other nonprofits to see what they are doing with their websites and advertising. Get on the mailing lists of several nonprofits, especially the planned giving mailing lists, and learn how they approach donors.

Of all the resources you have available, your database is your most valuable. Planned giving donors are notorious for camouflaging themselves deep in databases. Planned giving donors, for the most part, are quiet and rarely attract attention.

Scan your database, listen at meetings, and ask senior staff to be on the lookout for:

- Anyone who has given consistently for years. The amount is not as important as the frequency. People who give regularly and consistently believe in your mission. That belief is easily translatable to a planned gift. People who give consistently want to make a planned gift. They need only know they can.

- Anyone, but especially older donors, who say things like, "I wish I could give more, but don't know how," "I would give but I need the income," are all great candidates for gift annuities and bequest gifts.

- Anyone who complains about CD rates or the poor economy, are especially good candidates for gift annuities.

- Anyone who talks about a legacy or a desire to make an impact on the generations that follow.

Marketing

Whenever I go shopping for a car the salesman always insists on raising the hood and talking about the injection system, the intake and all kinds of things I have no knowledge or interest in learning. All I want to know is how reliable the car is, and maybe how efficient or possibly how powerful it is. Donors are the same.

Few donors care about the subtleties of trusts and gift annuities. Don't sell them on the ins and outs of the vehicle. Tell them how they can make a difference and how the vehicle will benefit them and their family. That's what they want to hear. That's what they need to know (but always be prepared with the details).

"No one ever listened himself out of a job."
– Calvin Coolidge.

Whether you are talking to one donor or a dozen, keep it simple. Keep it mission-focused. Donors do not really want to hear about gift annuities, trusts and wills. They *do want* to hear how they can make a difference; especially if they can do so with advantages they may not have known they had.

Focus on what your organization can do that the donor wishes he or she could do. Increase your concentration on the long-term benefits of giving to your organization. If your mission is to eliminate a disease, paint a picture what the world would be like without that disease. Always look for ways to show your donors you are here for the duration, and that they can trust their money to you and that you will be a good steward of their money tomorrow and forever.

Practice Listening

No one listens anymore. Everyone brags about his or her blogs, Facebook pages, and Twitter posts. The good fundraisers are those who follow more than they are followed.

When you can listen to what your donors are saying, you are well ahead of most fundraisers. Listening is the single-most important skill a fundraiser can have. Practice the art of active listening. Engage the donor and encourage the donor to open up about what is important in the donor's life.

When you are with donors, or talking to people you want to lead you to donors, ask open-ended questions. Avoid questions that can be answered with one word. Begin all or most of your questions with the words:

- Who,

- What,

- When,

- Where,

- and why.

Here are some questions you can ask any donor any time. Use them in context and with the right tone (gentle, caring, authentic) and the donor will *never* disappoint you with the answer.

- When did you first become interested in our organization?

- Why do you give so generously?

- What is the most important thing we do?

- Who should I get to know to help us build our cause?

- Where should I begin to reach out to donors in our planned giving efforts?

- What do you see as the future of our organization?

Even if the person you are talking to is the person you want to make the big gift, you can still ask for advice or insight. By asking a donor what motivates the donor you get not only the donor's advice, but insight into *that donor*.

*Nothing can take the place of getting out of
the office and seeing a donor face-to-face.*

A Potpourri of Ideas to Get Started

- Start a calendar of birth dates and important milestones in the lives of your donors. Send your donors birthday cards. Send them Thanksgiving cards (Christmas cards get lost in piles of mail and *Thanksgiving* is always an appropriate message for a nonprofit).

- If your donor's company went public on a certain date, send a congratulatory reminder on the anniversary. If you are a cancer charity and your donor was declared cancer-free on a certain date, be sure to celebrate it with the donor every year. Make donors feel special. Treat them as you would want to be treated. Love your donors and they will love you – and love your organization.

- Be authentic. Tell the truth. We live in a world where facts don't seem to feel as important as feelings. Level with your donor. Treat them as an insider, because they are. When donors sense they can trust you, you can trust them to open up generously. When you create a safe and truthful environment; anything is possible.

*The best way to encourage
donors to make a planned gift
is to make one ourselves.*

The 2% Rule

At your next board meeting, give a ten-minute presentation on charitable bequests and encourage each board member to include the organization in their plans. Challenge board members to make a gift of 2 percent in their wills or trusts to your cause.

A bequest gift will have zero impact on your board member's lifestyle, and no family member will ever complain when mom or dad made a gift of 2 percent to a cause that was dear enough to them that they served on the board.

Statistically half your board members have no will, so this is a good opportunity for them to provide for their families since it will prompt them to write their first will. A board member who will not give 2 percent in a will is a board member who does not believe in your cause. A board member who does not believe in your cause does not belong on your board.

It's a Trap!

Staff and well-meaning board members, like the friends in the *Wizard of Oz*, will encourage you to seek out the wealthy folks in town. "Go where the money is," they might say. While that may be fine, a better course is to read the book, *The Millionaire Next Door*. The book could just as easily be titled, *Your Planned Giving Donor Next Door*. Then *look* for the millionaires next door, **because few others are**.

I once heard from a wealthy donor about how people asked him for money. He said he would have at least one nonprofit contact him a week, sometimes many more. Each would walk in and present what they would believe to be a compelling case for him to make a large gift. He was amazed at how little homework they had done. Some asked for money for causes he would never support. Others did not respect his time and showed up unannounced on days before major corporate events or store openings (he owned a chain of grocery stores).

Still others misspelled his name. He might give them $100 just to make them go away. Eventually he received so many requests;

he developed a routine for quickly, but politely refusing them. Meanwhile, his mother who was just as wealthy, but less prolific was dying for attention and care, but no one called on her.

The Yellow Brick Road was wide and well trod to the top floors of the executive offices. The path to financial freedom was in the suburbs where few dared to venture.

The millionaires next door are everywhere, yet they live quiet, unassuming lives, carefully saving, carefully scrimping. They are the ones who give you $50 a year. They are the ones who can fund a $50,000 gift annuity or leave $1 million in their wills to you. But surprisingly, few nonprofits bother to talk with them.

The Only Offensive Planned Giving Message is the One not Asked

Avoid the negative Nellies. I have never heard from a donor who was offended by a planned giving message–never. A tasteful, appropriate message never offends. It just doesn't. People who believe in your mission are in it for the long haul, and distance drivers know you need to plan ahead.

The people who tell you not to bring planned giving messages to donors are not planned giving donors and never will be. They just "know better," on behalf of others.

Avoid these people and stick to what you know is right and true. If the naysayer is your supervisor or board chair, it is time to hope for a new leader, or you might consider pursuing a new position elsewhere. Leadership that does not understand planned giving is not the kind of leaders you want running your nonprofit organization.

As you feel the gears of your planned giving program start to produce momentum, build the infrastructure you will need to continue growing.

- Develop things like a gift acceptance policy that will help you and your nonprofit decide what planned gifts you will accept under what conditions.

- Develop a long-range communications plan that charts out what planned giving messages you want to send–and when.

- Improve your database by standardizing donor planned giving information especially as it relates to notes about visits and contacts.

- Find mentors at other nonprofits so you can compare notes and exchange ideas.

- Move forward with confidence that you have what it takes to make planned giving work for your organization, but there is always much more than can be done.

Think like a Donor, then Thank them, then Thank them Again

My parting advice to you comes from the title of my first book: *Think Like a Donor*. You would think we all think like donors, but too often, we don't. We think like nonprofits.

We think about our needs, our goals and our deadlines, and present donors a list of those and ask them to fulfill them for us. Sounds kind of harsh, but unfortunately, it is closer to reality than it should be.

Do what you do so well that they will want
to see it again and bring their friends. –
Walt Disney

The key to being a super fundraiser is to think like those we want to reach. What is important to Mrs. Smith today? Why has Mr. Jones given to us for so long and what might be holding him back from giving more? When Mr. Franklin sends us his gift in rolls of pennies what is he trying to tell us?

> People expect good service but few are
> willing to give it. – Robert Gateley

A nonprofit must always be aware of the emotions that led to the planned gift. Unlike direct gifts of cash, with most planned gifts the donor can change his or her mind. The emotions that led the donor to choose to give to you can also switch direction and provide ample reason not to give, too.

Be aware that just because a donor has committed to a planned gift, that is only the beginning. You are now in a life-long relationship with the donor, and if done properly with the donor's family as well.

Always look for ways to thank and acknowledge planned giving donors. Because planned gifts usually come to fruition after the donor has died, it is often difficult to figure out ways to honor a planned giving donor.

With a cash gift, you can name a building, a room, or a program after the donor. It's easy to quantify the gift and provide a venue of recognition appropriate to that amount.

Sadly, most charities ignore planned giving donors. The good news is if you honor your planned giving donors, your efforts will be appreciated even more, and perhaps your donor who was going to give to two or three causes will find herself wanting to give to only one: yours.

When we purposefully set out to engage donors and respond to their needs, our nonprofit enterprise will succeed. Planned giving gives donors the tools they need to make an incredible impact that they may not have thought possible. It also gives nonprofits much-needed support.

Planned giving need not be complicated. With a donor-centered approach and heart for the mission, your donors will give willingly and abundantly, and you will have the satisfaction of knowing you have done everything you can to support the mission that's important to both them and you.

To Recap:

- Planned Giving is about relationships.

- Practice active listening.

- Pay attention to the donors whom others ignore.

- Always thank your donors; then thank them again.

Appendix A Glossary

Actuary: A person who specializes in projecting lifespans of classes of people based on historic and statistical analysis.

Actuarial Tables: used in the work of actuaries, are important in the payment rates and tax calculations for gift annuities, charitable trusts and other split-interest gifts.

Adjusted Gross Income: The total income of an individual after any deductions are applied. There are various limits on deductions applied to gross income to arrive at the adjusted gross income figure.

Appraisal: A professional opinion as to the value of property. Appraisals are especially important to charitable planning when the gift is real property or an interest in it, or the property or asset is valued at $5,000 or more.

Appreciated Property: An asset that is worth more today than when its owner purchased it. Appreciated property is generally associated with discussion or disposition of investment assets such as stocks, bonds and real property. *See also*, Capital Gains.

Bargain Sale: The sale of an asset to a charity at a price less than the market value. The seller (who is also the donor) receives an income tax deduction for that portion of the sale price that is essentially a gift to the charity.

Basis: See, *Cost Basis*, below.

Beneficiary: The person or entity that is to receive or receives a distribution from a trust, will, life insurance policy or other planning instrument.

Bequest: A legal term generally describing that portion of a will directing the disposition of an asset owned by the decedent. In planned giving, bequests refer to gifts to a charity by will. You may also hear a bequest described as a "devise," and although improper or at best shorthand, some will say "will," or "codicil" when they mean "bequest." A bequest can be specific (e.g. $10,000, my 1953 Corvette) or a percentage (10% of my estate) or a remainder ("anything not specifically devised above.")

Capital Gains: The difference in value between the price one paid for an investment asset and the money received upon its sale. Capital gains occur when the asset has appreciated in value. Capital losses occur when the asset has depreciated in value.

Charitable Bequest: A sentence, paragraph or clause in a person's will giving an asset to a charity.

Charitable Gift Annuity: An irrevocable contract between a charity and a donor or donors where the charity agrees to pay one or two people (beneficiaries) of the donor's choosing a fixed amount each year for as long as the beneficiary or beneficiaries live. The payment rate is usually based on rates published by the American Council on Gift Annuities and is dependent on the beneficiary's or beneficiaries' ages. After all payments to the beneficiary or beneficiaries, the remainder becomes available for use by the charity. There are several varieties of gift annuities such as the deferred gift annuity, college gift annuity, and flexible deferred gift annuity. State and federal laws govern gift annuities.

Charitable Lead Trust: The complement to the unitrust, the lead trust pays a percentage of trust assets to a charity or charities during the life of the trust, then after the term of the trust, trust assets are distributed to the donor, or beneficiaries of the donor's choosing. Tax benefits vary with the donor's choice of beneficiaries.

Charitable Remainder Annuity Trust: Also known as a CRAT, like a unitrust, except the CRAT pays a fixed amount each year rather than a percentage of trust assets.

Charitable Remainder Unitrust: Also known as a CRUT or Unitrust, this is an irrevocable transfer of assets from a donor or donors to a trust. The duration of the trust is measured by a term of years or by the lives of designated people. The trust pays a percentage of its assets each year to designated beneficiaries during the life of the trust. At the termination of the trust any remaining funds are transferred free of the trust to the charity or charities designated by the donor when the donor established the trust. Unitrusts have many varieties including the FLIP Unitrust, Charitable Remainder Trust with Net Income Makeup (NIMCRUT) and others.

Codicil: A revision to a will by adding to it. The form and validity of a codicil is governed by state law, and must comply with the same formalities and requirements as if it were the original will.

Commercial Annuity: A contractual agreement, usually between an insurance company and an individual, where the individual gives the company a sum of money in exchange for the company's agreement to pay a fixed sum of money to the individual at regular intervals. A gift annuity is not a commercial annuity, but shares some characteristics such as regular interval payments.

Contingent Bequest: A bequest that is dependent on some other event happening or not happening. "I leave $100 to ABC Charity if my children do not survive me."

Cost Basis: The cost basis, or basis, is how much someone paid for an investment asset. The cost basis in stock is the price the buyer paid for it. When the stock owner sells it for more than the owner paid for it, the owner has experienced a capital gain and pays capital gains tax on the difference between the sales price and the cost basis. When the asset sells for less than what the owner paid for it, it is a capital loss and generally may be used to offset capital gains realized from the sale of other assets the same year.

Death Tax: See Estate Tax, below.

Endowment: Also known as an Endowment Fund is an investment fund owned by a charity. Generally the principal of the fund is never spent and the appreciation or income from the fund is used to further the mission of the organization. Organizations typically designate a spending formula for the fund, for example, 4% of the total average value of the fund over the last three years (so a particularly good or bad investment year does not skew annual expenditures).

Estate Tax: A federal tax, also known as a Death Tax, on the value of property owned by an individual at death. The estate pays this tax before making distributions to family and other beneficiaries. One of the great values of planned giving is that certain charitable planning vehicles remove assets from the estate, thus lessening the amount in the estate that would otherwise be taxable. Funds not part of the estate are not subject to the estate tax. Individual states also may impose an inheritance tax on estates. Like the estate tax, inheritance taxes are paid by the estate and not beneficiaries.

Executor: See, *Personal Representative*, below.

Fair Market Value: This is an estimate of what a willing buyer would pay to a willing seller in a free market for a certain asset.

Form 8282: An official IRS form, known as the Donee Information Return, also known as the Tattletale Form. The IRS states its purpose is for donee organizations to report information to the IRS and donors about dispositions of certain charitable deduction property made within 3 years after the donor contributed the property. If the charity does anything other than keep the donated property within 3 years after the donation, the charity must file this form with the IRS. As of the date of publication of this book, the form applies to assets valued by the donor at $5,000 or more. See also, Form 8283.

Form 8283: An official IRS form, also known as the "Noncash Charitable Contributions Form." The IRS requires the form to be completed by the donor with the donor's income tax return for all noncash gifts to charity. Donations of $500 or less require basic information about the gift. Donations between $500 and $5,000 require more detail, while donations of $5,000 or more require a qualified appraisal. The rules governing Form 8283 and Form 8282 are strict and strictly interpreted by the IRS and are subject to frequent revision. *Whenever you solicit or accept noncash gifts (other than some stocks) be sure to consult with experienced, qualified professionals.*

Gift Planning: A synonym for Planned Giving.

Grantor: A legal term for the person (donor) who establishes a trust.

Income Beneficiary: The person or entity receiving income payouts from a trust during the trust's existence.

Income Interest: A term used to describe the right to receive payments from a trust.

Instrument: The contract, account, will or document used to convey an idea, asset or property from one party to another. A trust, for example, is an instrument that allows a donor to give to charity and receive payments.

Intestate: Adjective describing one who dies without a will.

Form 1099-R: An IRS form that charities use to send payment information each January to beneficiaries of gift annuities and pooled income funds to show the amount and character of payments made the prior year. (The form

166

shows not only total payments, but also how much of each was principal, capital gains and income).

Issue: A legal term for children. For example, a person without children is, "without issue."

Life Expectancy: An actuarial estimate of how much longer an individual has to live based on the person's age and other societal statistics.

Liquid: An asset that can be sold in a relatively brief period of time. Stocks and bonds are generally liquid because their value is relatively easy to determine at any given time. Real estate, cars, diamonds and some other assets are "illiquid," because the market for them varies a little more, and a buyer must be found.

Non-cash Asset: Any asset such as securities, life insurance, CDs, bonds, etc., that is of value but is not cash. Cash or cash-equivalent assets are currency, checks, and gifts using credit cards.

Personal Property: Property that can be moved or touched. Anything owned other than real property. This includes planes, cars, jewelry, artwork, and any other asset that can be touched. For this reason, "personal property," is also often referred to as "tangible personal property."

Personal Representative: A modern term for the executor or executrix of an estate. The personal representative is the person named in a will to administer the estate. If no personal representative is named, or if that person is no longer able to serve, the probate court may appoint a personal representative.

Planned Gift (or planned giving): Also known as a "deferred gift," includes any gift other than cash or a check. The concept of a planned gift started with gifts that usually came to fruition upon the happening of a certain event, usually death of the donor, or the passage of time (after a set number of years). Planned giving has grown to include other types of giving, notably in-kind gifts, such as artwork, vehicles, jewelry, collectibles and real estate. Planned gifts include gifts of stock. The most common planned gifts are by will, gift annuity, trust, life insurance or retirement accounts.

Present Value: The value of an asset today. When an asset is promised to be given to a charity at some future date, its present value represents the asset's worth today. A gift of $1 promised a year from now is worth less than a gift of $1 today. Inflation, investment risk and other factors all affect an asset's value today when compared to its value in the future. Present value is often described in connection with the "time value of money," which expresses the concept that the same amount of money has different actual values depending on when one owns it or is promised it.

Probate: The division of the state court system responsible for administering the wills of decedents (dead people). Among other responsibilities, the Probate Court ensures the will is authentic and assets are distributed properly.

Real Property: A legal term that refers to land and the ownership of it. It includes the buildings and fixtures on the property. Real estate and real property generally refer to the same concept, at least for gifting purposes.

Related Use: The concept that something tangible given to a charity will be given to the charity for use related to the mission of the organization. For example, a gift of artwork to an art museum for display in the museum would generally be considered a "related use." A donation of the artwork to a zoo (which does not display art) would be an "unrelated use." See §170(e)(1)(i), Internal Revenue Code. A gift of an appreciated property for a related use generally qualifies for a higher income tax deduction than a gift of appreciated property for an unrelated use.

Remainder Beneficiary: The person or entity receiving assets from a trust after the termination of the trust's existence.

Remainder Bequest: A bequest of anything not devised by other parts of the will. A remainder might also be called "residue."

Remainder Interest: The trust assets available for distribution to a person, persons, entity, or entities as specified by the trust at the termination of the trust. Those receiving payments from the trust during the term of the trust are those with an "Income Interest," or are life beneficiaries.

Remaindermen: A legal term specifying the person, people, entity or entities the grantor of the trust designated to receive the trust principal or remainder when the trust terminates.

Securities: Another way of saying "stock." Generally used to describe shares in a publicly traded corporation. Securities are liquid, meaning they can be sold for cash reasonably quickly on the open market.

Split-Interest Gift: A gift to a charity where the donor retains some aspect of ownership or control over a portion of the gift. The "split" refers to the fact that the donor and charity now each have an interest in the ownership, outcome or control of the asset. Unitrusts, gift annuities and life estates are all examples of split-interest gifts.

Term Life Insurance: Life Insurance with a duration measured in a term of years rather than the life of the insured.

Testamentary: Something created by a will. A testamentary trust, for example, is a trust created by a donor in the donor's will. The trust did not exist before the person died. An intervivos trust is a trust created during the grantor's life.

Testate: One who dies with a will.

Testator: The person making a will.

Trust: A legal entity created by a written instrument by a grantor or donor to own and invest property for the benefit of those named in the trust.

Trustee: An individual or organization responsible for carrying out the terms of the trust.

Whole Life Insurance: Life insurance that pays a benefit upon the death of the insured.

Appendix B Helpful Resources

Crescendointeractive.com – a website for planned giving calculations, publications help, education and website development. Crescendo provides training at its headquarters in California and at a national Practical Planned Giving Conference each fall.

Pgcalc.com – a website for planned giving calculations, education, and gift annuity information. It publishes a gift annuity handbook that is especially helpful in their marketing and administration.

Rrnewkirk.com – A planned giving publisher that also provides a thorough planned giving resource: The Charitable Giving Tax Service. It provides planned giving training twice a year in Chicago and at St. Pete Beach, Florida.

Sharpenet.com – A planned giving services firm that provides training, publications, and services for planned giving professionals.

Acga-web.org – the official website of the American council on Gift Annuities.

Irs.gov – the official website of the IRS and the source of helpful publications such as Publication 526 and other official forms.

Afpnet.org – the official website of the Association of Fundraising Professionals.

Wayneolson.com – My website. If you need to reach me, have ideas for improving future editions of this book or ideas for future publications, I can always be reached here, or at wayneolson@me.com

Studio 29·11 Katie Roussel, (if you like the cover design and layout and are looking for an excellent artist). http://www.linkedin.com/pub/katie-casler/23/7b3/83a/

Index

B

C

CRUT, 95, 98, 100, 164

CRUTS, 87

D

Deferred gift annuities, 72

disclosure letter, 78

E

Elbert Hubbard, 149

Electronic transfer, 30

Environmental, 124, 125

estate plan, 23, 45, 46, 47, 51, 88

Estate Tax, 37, 38, 165

estate taxes, 37, 40, 41, 89

F

Farm land, 117

farms, 24, 125

Federal Express, 30

federal tax code, 32

FLIP Unitrust, 99, 164

font, 53

forests, 24

Form 8282, 109, 110, 165, 166

Form 8283, 107, 109, 110, 111, 112, 114, 166

Four-tier Approach, 96

G

Generation Skipping Tax, 39

gift tax, 37, 38, 39

H

homes, 24, 106, 125, 149

I

illustration, 64, 66, 73, 75

income tax, 28, 29, 35, 36, 41, 60, 64, 65, 71, 74, 75, 76, 80, 93, 94, 95, 96, 97, 102, 109, 110, 112, 113, 118, 119, 121, 122, 128, 130, 133, 139, 140, 141, 162, 166, 168

In-Kind, 109

Insurance, 23, 61, 132, 133, 134, 135, 136, 137, 169, 170

Intangible, 104, 107, 113

Intellectual Property, 113

IRA, 137, 138, 139, 140, 141, 142

IRA rollover, 138, 140, 141

irrevocable bequests, 46

J

jewelry, 24, 72, 106, 167, 168

John Frey, 59

L

L. Frank Baum, 144

Lewis Carol, 44

Long Term Capital Gains, 96

M

Marketing, 78, 152

Method of Gift, 30

Mortgage, 120

N

O

P

R